Library of
Davidson College

Anthony Trollope's
Son in Australia

Anthony Trollope's Son in Australia

THE LIFE AND LETTERS OF
F.J.A. TROLLOPE (1847–1910)

P.D. Edwards

University of Queensland Press
St Lucia • London • New York

© University of Queensland Press, St Lucia, Queensland 1982

This book is copyright. Apart from any fair dealing for the purposes of private study, research, criticism, or review, as permitted under the Copyright Act, no part may be reproduced by any process without written permission. Enquiries should be made to the publishers.

Typeset by University of Queensland Press
Printed and bound by Hedges & Bell Pty Ltd, Melbourne

Distributed in the United Kingdom, Europe, the Middle East, Africa, and the Caribbean by Prentice-Hall International, International Book Distributors Ltd, 66 Wood Lane End, Hemel Hempstead, Herts., England.

National Library of Australia
Cataloguing-in-Publication data

Edwards, P.D. (Peter David), 1931–
    Anthony Trollope's son in Australia.

ISBN 0 7022 1891 X.

1 Trollope, F.J.A. (Frederic James Anthony), 1847–1910. 2. Australia – Description and travel – 1851–1891. I. Trollope, F.J.A. (Frederic James Anthony), 1847–1910. II. Title.

919.4'043'0924

Library of Congress Cataloguing in Publication Data

Edwards, Peter David.
    Anthony Trollope's son in Australia.

1. Trollope, F.J.A. (Frederic James Anthony), 1847–1910. 2. Trollope, Anthony, 1815–1882 — Biography. 3. Trollope family. 4. Australia — Biography. I. Trollope, F.J.A. (Frederic James Anthony), 1847–1910. II. Title.
PR5686.E33   823'.8[B]   82-4928
ISBN 0-7022-1891-X   AACR2

Acknowledgments

I am grateful to Professor N. John Hall who told me of the University of Illinois' collection of manuscript letters from Frederic Trollope to his parents and his brother Harry. I also thank Mrs Mary Ceibert of the Rare Book Room, University of Illinois Library at Urbana-Champaign, for supplying me with a microfilm of the letters and the library itself for permitting me to print them.

In my research, and in the preparation of this little book, I have received valuable assistance from Sue Thomas, Margaret Dawson, and the staff of the University of Queensland Library, the National Library of Australia, the Public Library of New South Wales, and the Mitchell Library.

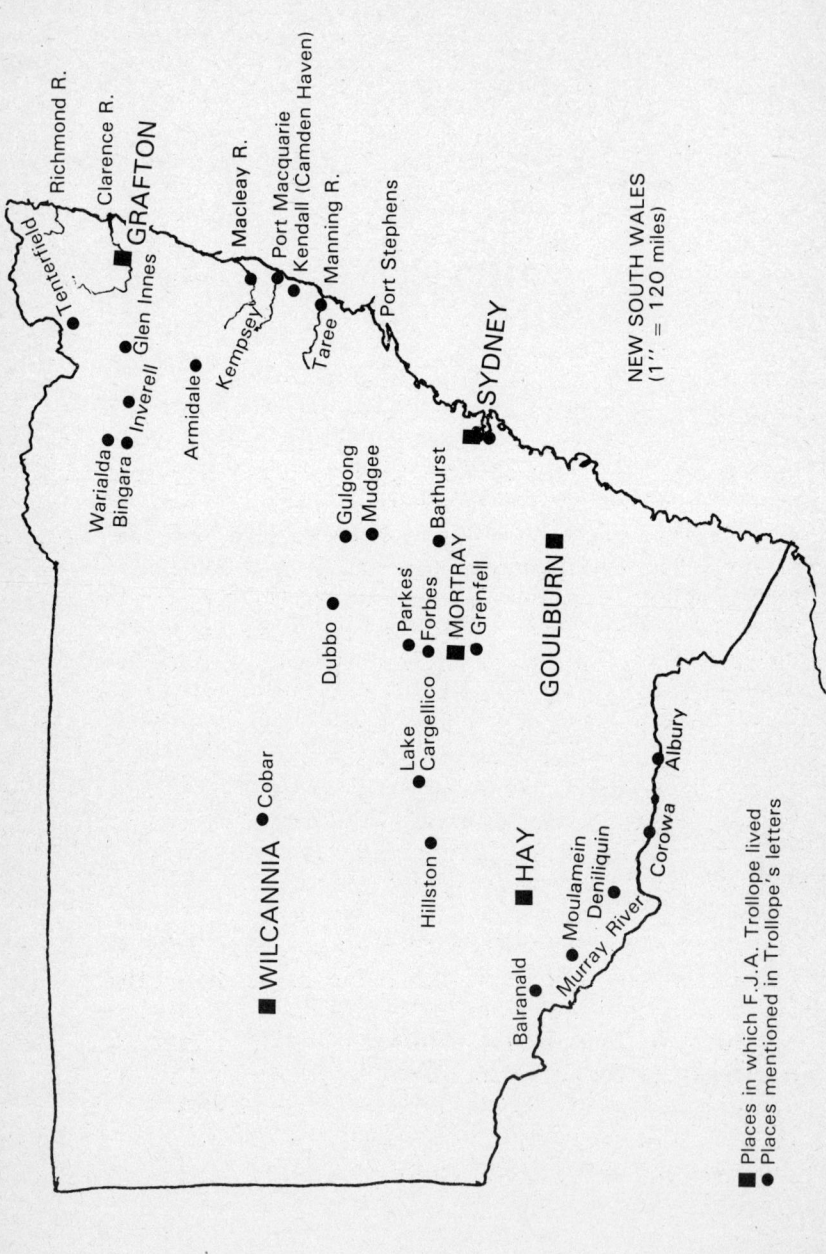

Anthony Trollope's Son in Australia

On Saturday, 25 April 1885, a certain Morgan D'Arcy was charged in the Police Court at Wilcannia with cruelty to animals. Two witnesses deposed that D'Arcy had brutally lashed four horses attached to a buggy, while another man was seated in the buggy applying the brake and holding the horses back with all his strength. The contest between the two men had taken place outside the Mount Murchison hotel and had evidently resulted from a bet made in the hotel bar. After hearing several witnesses, the magistrates dismissed the charge on grounds of insufficient evidence. A week later the *Wilcannia Times*, which had reported the case, ran a lengthy editorial castigating the magistrates' finding as a gross miscarriage of justice.

Two of the leading actors in this little scene of frontier life were Frederic James Anthony Trollope, who was chief prosecution witness, and Edward Bulwer Lytton Dickens, who was one of the police magistrates.

The astonishing coincidence that made the younger son of Anthony Trollope and the youngest of Charles Dickens fellow-citizens of a tiny township on the Darling River, five hundred miles inland from Sydney, is recorded in Mary Lazarus's *A Tale of Two Brothers*, which charts the Australian careers of Alfred Tennyson D'Orsay Dickens and E.B.L. ("Plorn") Dickens.[1] Fred Trollope and Plorn Dickens both played a leading part in Wilcannia life, and Plorn's long period of residence there, culminating in his sitting as member for the district in the New South Wales parliament (1889-94), was the one bright spot in his life in Australia. Before going into parliament he ran a stock and station agency in partnership with his brother (who conducted the Melbourne branch); both he and Fred Trollope were honorary magistrates, parochial councillors, and members of local cricket clubs; Plorn was also a senior official of the Jockey and Lawn Tennis clubs, and Fred, as a member of the Athenaeum Committee, was responsible for ordering books for the town library. But life in Wilcannia cannot have been easy even for leading citizens. The mayor, who was proprietor and editor of the *Wilcannia Times* and, like Plorn Dickens, an auctioneer and honorary magistrate, had suddenly to vacate all his offices because of bankruptcy; his successor as mayor was accused of adultery with a neighbour's wife and failed to sustain a charge of slander against his accusers; an alderman was gaoled for four months for beating his wife; and even townspeople whose business and marital concerns were better ordered could not escape the extreme heat or the piles of sand that blocked their doorways in the morning. Certainly Fred Trollope, who had had plenty of experience of the discomforts of outback life, seems to have considered Wilcannia the worst of many unpleasant places to which his work took him: his description of it, in a letter to his family back home in England, put his uncle in mind of the lines, "Out of humanity's reach/He must finish his battle alone".[2]

However gloomy Fred's view of his plight at this time, it was incomparably less grim than that which overtook the Dickens brothers in the 1890s, when their business seems to have collapsed and Plorn lost his seat in parliament; and there was no disaster in Fred's private life to parallel the tragic accident in which Alfred Dickens's first wife was killed. In its apparent uneventfulness, its lack of spectacular and decisive reverses of fortune, its gently but persistently thwarted hopes, Fred's career resembles a Trollope novel; it was a steady, decent, mildly prosperous life, and its frustrations and inconveniences were endured with fortitude, though not always with exemplary patience. Fred was too conservative and too proud to have risked compromising his dignity and self-sufficiency as the Dickens brothers did. There is no trace in him of the tendency to ostentation, raffishness, even seediness that we can hardly fail to perceive in them. Both he and they are their fathers' sons. But Fred's story, like theirs, is interesting not only for this reason but also for the vivid illustration it provides of the rawness and hardness of colonial life — even for people with education and money — in the last third of the nineteenth century and the first decade of the twentieth.

* * * * *

The main sources of information about Frederic Trollope's life in Australia are a long obituary in the Hay newspaper, the *Riverine Grazier*, on 7 June 1910, and the twenty-six letters to his family, now in the possession of the University of Illinois library, which are printed below. Most of the letters were written to his mother — who outlived him — but there are also several to his father, who died in 1882, and two to his elder brother Henry (Harry). Other family letters and papers in the same library, chiefly letters to Harry from his uncle, Thomas Adolphus Trollope, throw occasional light on Fred, and there are of course references to him in his father's *Autobiography* (1883) and published letters (*The Letters of Anthony Trollope*, ed. Bradford Allen Booth, O.U.P., 1951). He is also mentioned, though not by name, in his father's travel-book *Australia and New Zealand* (1873), especially in chapter 20, "Country Life in the Bush". R.B. Joyce and I included a largely conjectural sketch of his colonial career in the introduction to our edition of the Australian sections of this book (Trollope's *Australia*, University of Queensland Press, 1967, pp. 18-20): the Illinois letters and the obituary in the *Riverine Grazier* show that most of our conjectures were wide of the mark. There are some minor errors, chiefly with regard to dates, in the obituary, but much of it consists of personal recollections that must have been supplied by Frederic Trollope himself, or just conceivably by a member of his family.

Fred was born on 27 September 1847, so that, as the obituary points out, he was "just eighteen" when he reached Melbourne on 17 December 1865.[3] According to Anthony Trollope's *Autobiography*, Fred had decided on a colonial career because "boys who did not grow so fast as he did got above him at school".[4] The obituary in the *Riverine Grazier*,[5] however, asserted that his masters "wished him to matriculate at Cambridge, with a view to taking a degree in mathematics", but he had made up his mind when he was only fifteen to "try his fortune in Australia". His school, Bradfield near Reading ("a fair type of the smaller English public school"), was noted for sports and Fred won "a fair share of athletic prizes": in Australia he, and later some of his sons, were leading lights in cricket in all the bush towns where most of his life was spent. After three years in Australia, first at Barratta Station near Deniliquin, then in Victoria, he returned to England just after his twenty-first birthday. There he was to decide, in accordance with a previous agreement with his parents, whether to remain in England or return to Australia. His father reports, in his *Autobiography* (p. 326), that although Fred made the most of the hunting season while at home, there was "no doubt in his own mind as to his settling in Australia". He arrived back in Melbourne on 12 July 1869[6] and shortly after bought Mortray, a small sheep station near Grenfell in New South Wales. His parents came out to Australia in 1871-72, his father spending a few weeks at Mortray in October-November 1871 and a few more in June 1872. At the time the 27,500 acre property carried 10,000 sheep. Fred was still living on it "in the rough" but had completed forty miles of fencing at a cost of £25 a mile. During his parents' visit — on 14 December 1871 — he married Susannah Farrand, daughter of the police magistrate at Forbes; but his parents, presumably because Anthony had prior commitments in Victoria at about the same time, did not attend the wedding.[7]

The first of Fred's letters in the University of Illinois collection would have reached his mother soon after she and Anthony arrived back in England. It begins with an account of the health of his eldest son, who had been born on Fred's birthday, 27 September 1872.

Letter 1   **Mortray**   **24 November 1872**

My dear Mother

I hope to hear of you soon from San Francisco, but the mails to & from there seem to be so very irregular that there is no depending on them.

You will have seen in my last letter all about Frank. He seems to be getting on well & growing a big fellow. He was a very small baby when he was born & woe-fully thin, but he is mending all that now. I got over my shearing in good time this year & was able to keep my sheep free from grass seed. I shall be glad to hear from you when you get home, all about your — — — [?] voyage & stay in California, also about your trip across the continent. I should think you must have found the long railway journey very irksome & fatiguing.

You have no idea how scarce labor is getting to be in Australia at all events in N.S.W. There are so many men mining now. Not only gold mining but tin & copper take away a great many men. This year shearers were very scarce at the beginning & as the time went on they got more & more scarce. I began with ten & at the start discharged two, & during the whole time I was unable to get any more. I was certainly lucky in getting together a very good lot of men much better than those I got when you & my Father were at Mortray.

At the end of shearing I was obliged to send away my cook and though I have got a *maid* girl since then I have been unable to get a *man*. Then Bridget, Susie's girl left us to go & get married, & for the last fortnight Susie has had to do almost every thing herself. Now she has just got another girl & such a specimen of a wild beast you never saw. Susie is trying to teach her, but I am afraid it is a hopeless job. I am now getting in my crop of hay. I will have a very heavy crop. I have cut about a quarter of it, & I am afraid that a good deal of that cut will be spoiled for it has rained ever since it has been cut so that it is impossible to get it dried. It has indeed been a most curious season. We are having even more rain now than there was in the winter.

There has been a good deal of excitement about here lately, on account of a murder on a neighbouring station.[8] There are several men implicated, two among them are men who have been working at Mortray. One is a very decent looking fellow — you might recolect him, he was making those chairs my Father was recomending for the verandah — the other was our handy. It seems to have been a horrible affair, the murdered man was found all mangled & burned. There seems to be no evidence in the case whatever except the evidence of the men implicated & every one of them has a different yarn of his own, each accusing the others & exonerating himself.

About a week ago Susie had a letter from Powell & he says he is engaged to be married to a Miss Maccabbie [?] daughter of a Doctor in Bathurst. I believe she is older than Powell, not pretty & Susie who used to know her says not at all nice. However I suppose Powell is the best judge of all that. Powell says nothing of Isabella or of Mark though I asked him to let me know how they were getting on. The chances are they are doing well. Hill End has got to be a very busy place, & a smart hard working fellow like Mark would have a good chance.

I wonder where you will live when you get home? If Harry has taken a comfortable place for you. Let me know what has been done with the old house, or what is to be done with it.[9]

The telegrams from England have been reporting money as being very tight at home. That of course greatly influences the price of wool out here.

I enclose you a scrap of Original Poetry from that great paper The Forbes Times — it is very pretty & sentimental. I shall be so glad to get an odd English paper — The Saturday or something of that sort, when you get home. A fellow out here loses sight of every thing that is going on, & then when you hear things talked about you dont know where you are. Since you have been away from England I seem to have lost sight of pretty nearly every body there. It seems to me as if I had not heard anything of anybody in England for an age.

As I was coming up to Mortray from Melbourne, Young Dickens went down. Since that he has got some position in that old company of Cloughs under that B— — G— —* — Papa will know who I mean. I cant say I envy him his billet. I am sorry though that he has left the district, as it makes one neighbour the less with whome you can exchange an idea. By the way we had a great calling on Mrs Boland the other day & all climbed up the Bald Hills. You get from there by far the finest view I have seen in this part of the country. I must now say good bye. Susie was to have written by this mail but she is very busy & has to defer her letter to next mail. Love to all at home.

Your very affectionate son
Fred Trollope

Tell Harry I was asking after him — He is not out here yet.

The plentiful rain that produced such a heavy crop of hay in 1872 did not repeat itself in subsequent seasons.

I have not been able to identify "Powell", "Isabella" or "Mark", but Fred and his family had evidently known them in England.

The note of homesickness in Fred's second last paragraph seldom recurs: his parents' departure had no doubt reminded him that his exile would now almost certainly be permanent and irrevocable, and in fact it was to be more than thirty years before he visited England again. Later letters make it clear that his parents did do their best to keep him in touch with home by sending the "odd English paper" — *Blackwood's Magazine* for example, and presumably the *Saturday Review* too. His remark that the departure of "Young Dickens" made one neighbour the less with whom he could exchange an idea was probabaly an understatement. This was not the future police magistrate at Wilcannia but his elder brother, Alfred Tennyson D'Orsay Dickens, who had visited Mortray during Anthony Trollope's stay there in June 1872.[10] The firm

---

* Name illegible.

that he was about to begin working for in Melbourne — having sold his property near Mortray — was I.H. Clough and Co., who had acted as Anthony's agents during part of his stay in Australia. There is no evidence that Alfred's and Fred's paths ever crossed again.

Letter 2   **Mortray**   **29 November 1872**

My dear Harry

I have a kind of an idea that you & I are not keeping up the regular correspondence we used to at one time. I believe I must plead guilty to being the first towards dropping it. I suppose you heard all about the arrival of your young nephew Frank Anthony Trollope into the world about eight weeks ago. In fact he was born upon my birth day.

At first he seemed inclined to be very weak & delicate but now he seems to be growing a strong little fellow. But I will not discant upon his merits. I will let Susie do that for I suppose she is like all other mothers & thinks there is no baby in the world like her own.

Susie got a letter from Powell the other day saying that he was engaged to be married to a Bathurst young lady, one Miss Maccabbie [?], who seems, as far as I can gather, to be chiefly distinguished by having at different times been engaged to every single man in the district. She is older than Powell, & not pretty, & has I believe no money. And as Powell has none I expect it will be a long engagement. I should not at all wonder if it ends in smoke, as I said before the girl is used to that sort of thing. However dont hint anything of that sort to Powells friends in England. Powell is a very nice fellow & I should like to see him get a nice wife.

All the world in Australia has been mad upon mining. It was realy quite ridiculous, you would meet a fellow you knew — "How do Jones —" "Good day Smith" "Look here what do you think of this" — & he would produce a piece of stone supposed to contain gold, copper, tin, or some infernal metal or another — "Not bad" the other would say, "but what do you think of this". Then another infernal specimen would be produced.

I realy believe I am the only person for fifty miles round

about that is not a shareholder in some company, or some mineral selection or lease or some blessed thing to do with mining. They are all going to make their fortunes — some day. There is no doubt that mining is beginning to be a large industry in N.S.W. & that in a few years time she will exporte more gold than Victoria.

In Victoria they were much more go-ahead & quickly adopted good modes of working large mines by machinery. That they are only just beginning to do in New South Wales now.

In NSW the gold fields are much more scattered than they are in Victoria. They are at great distances apart & a long way from the sea coast. I am trying to sell my wool in Sydney this year. There is always a certain risk in shipping it that some unforseen event may produce a fall in the market.

The way I do, I determine as nearly as I can the value of the wool. I put a reserve upon it, if it will clear that I sell in Sydney, if not I ship it to London.

Good bye old Fellow, I hope to hear from you by next mail
Your very affect. Brother
Fred Trollope
I enclose Mama a specimen of Australian Poetry — read it & pass it on — it is the production of a Lawyer in Forbes.

This letter, covering much the same ground as the one to his mother only a few days before, was obviously inspired by the surge of homesickness that followed his parents' departure. Despite his proposal that he and Harry resume regular correspondence, only one other letter to Harry, written fourteen years later, seems to have survived. Others may well have passed between them but not been kept. Letter 2 probably survives because, like Fred's letters to her and to his father, it was kept by his mother: for by the time it reached England Harry was probably aboard the *Mooltan* on his way to Australia. Fred's postscript to Letter 1 ("Tell Harry I was asking after him — He is not out here yet") implies that he had been promised a visit from Harry for some time, but in the event the visit was obviously decided upon quite abruptly — and not because of Harry's sudden yearning for his brother's company. In 1869 Harry's father had bought him a third share in the distinguished publishing house of Chapman and Hall. But during his parents' absence in Australia he had fallen in love with a French actress in Paris. Upon their return he greeted them with the news that he intended to marry her. His father's response, characteristically peremptory, was to pack him off to Venice to board the *Mooltan* en route to Australia. The story, which may have been magnified slightly by gossip, is related in two letters of G.H. Lewes.[11] Harry arrived in Sydney on 21 February 1873 and left on 12 July.[12] Soon after his return to England he withdrew himself and his capital from Chapman and Hall and went to live on the Continent — with the French actress for company, let us hope.

Anthony Trollope's visit to Australia resulted in a novel about squatters and free selectors, *Harry Heathcote of Gangoil*.[13] The hero, a squatter, was based on Fred. Like Fred he was born in 1847 and emigrated to Australia at the age of seventeen because he was backward at school. He too has a baby son and is a magistrate (as Fred was from September 1872). Harry is hard-working and, except when crossed, good-humoured, but he also has a reputation for arrogance, for being "too imperious, too masterful, too much inclined to think that all things should be made to go as he would have them". That Fred shared these qualities is amply borne out by his letters.

As his father insisted, however, it was through no fault of Fred's own that he failed at Mortray and that what was perhaps the most hopeful period of his life came to an end. The property, which was merged with a neighbouring run in 1885, was too small and Fred's capital too limited to enable him to survive the prolonged drought that followed the good rains of 1872. During a second visit from his father (June–August 1875), it was evidently decided that Mortray would have to be sold. Fred's next letters inform his father of his financial position following the sale.

Letter 3   **Australian Club (Sydney)**   **12 January 1876**

My dear Father

I wrote you a few days ago by the Torres Straits mail, saying that I would write you again from Sydney giving you full particulars of my money affairs.

The result is this that after the cash payments (Rand payed more than half cash) Gilchrist Watt & co. have a claim of £2200 12s 10d on the station, against which there are two promissory notes of Rands secured by mortgage on the station.

	s	d
One due 4 October 1876	£1156 - 12.	0
One due 4 October 1877	£2498 - 6.	10
	£3654 - 18.	10
That stands against	2200 12.	10
Leaving in my favour	1454 6.	0

That is if the bills are left to be matured, & nothing is drawn against them. But I suppose it would cost me £250 to discount them. I think it would be the best thing to let the bills mature & try & obtain an advance against them. I believe I could get the £2200 12s 10d to pay off Watt & £1000 besides.

I have called at the Bank of N.S.W. but could not see Mr Shepherd Smith.[14] I saw the other man we saw together, & have since then written a letter to the manager enclosing my a/c with Watt & asking what sum I could draw against the bills for. I will see Smith, & will send you further particulars by the Suez mail.

Watt has been even more shark like than the Melbourne corporation. Though he had nothing to do with the sale & I had to pay £120 for sale commission to other parties, he charges me £129 & some odd shillings for his commission.

If you recolect he gave us, in a conversation distinctly to understand that in case he made no sale he would charge no commission.

I have spoken to one or two people about it, & they tell me his claim is quite unfounded.

Gilchrist Watt have a good name & the corporation in Melbourne had a bad one. But in looking over the accounts & comparing them together Watts charges for wool sales are always higher. Unless I find that some clause in the mortgage, compells me to pay them commission I shall dispute their claim.

I have been twice to Watt's office since I have been in Sydney, & each time he seemed to think the shorter the intervue [?] the better.

I have not seen Mr Kater since I have been down. I was talking yesterday to Mr. Hay,[15] & was telling him that I had heard of a small place on the Warrego. It is close to some stations of his, & he was giving me some particulars about it. He says the country is very good.

I should prefer to go into something larger than my own means would let me as a managing partner, even if my share was but a small one.

But when a man is looking about for what he wants he is spending his money. However it is well to get one thing settled before another is commenced, & till I know what I can do about the Mortray money affairs & have seen Smith of course I can do nothing.

While I have been writing to you Mr Dally has come into the room & desires to be remembered to you, & says he hopes to see you again some day.[16] I was at Government House yesterday & the Robinsons were very kind.

I called to tell Sir Hercules that I had sold Mortray & how I stood. They were all well & told me they had heard of you from Sir George Bowen.

I write again by Suez.
Your very affectionate son
Fred Trollope

On the back of this letter Anthony Trollope wrote a note to his elder son:

Dear Harry. I send this, as perhaps you will like to see it. The loss of money has been lamentable — over £4,600!! But it is a kind of misfortune which I can bear. Let me have the letter back.

Yours ever,
A.T.

Poor dear Fred. Do not suppose from what I have said on the other side that I blame him.

In his *Autobiography* (p. 348), Anthony lamented that "several thousand pounds which I had squeezed out of the pockets of perhaps too liberal publishers" were lost on Mortray; but he added: "I rejoice to say that this has been in no way due to any fault of [Fred's]. I never saw a man work with more persistent honesty at his trade".

Sir George Bowen, from whom the governor of New South Wales, Sir Hercules Robinson, had heard news of Anthony Trollope, was the governor of Victoria and had met the novelist during his first visit to Australia in 1871–72. Their more recent meeting had taken place in America, when Anthony was on his way home after his second (1875) visit.

Letter 4   **Sydney**   **16 January 1876**

My dear Father

I have now full particulars of Watt's account. I send you a coppy as they at first made out. I mark X an item which they charge for commission. It is altogether unjust as they distinctly said they would not charge if they did not make a sale. Again if they had any claim to com: they should have claimed it before letting me pay £131 to another party, as I advised them that I was so doing. I remonstrated & Watt said he would rebate one third. That was three or four days ago.

I saw a lawyer about it, & his advice was remonstrate against it, & if you have to pay do so under protest. I saw Watt again after that & again said I thought the charge ought not be made. All that he said was it was the usual custom. I then told him I would contest that item. Some hours after I got a letter saying that as I intended to dispute their account they would hand me another one in which instead of £129-4-6 commission (E.F. [?] at the rate of 1½) they would charge £215-7-6 (=2½) as such was stipulated in their mortgage.

I shall get sufficient money from Rands bills to pay them their claim. The extra £215-7-6 I will pay under protest & I do not doubt that I shall be able to recover it. According to Watt, his charge is only fixed by his own rapacity, & he had only to demand, 5, 10 or 50 per cent & deduct if from the account.

As I told you I could not see Smith at the Bank of N.S.W. when I called first time, neither could I see him when I called again. Neither could I get a deffinite answer. I want Watt to be paid off, at all events, or he will be bringing in some other iniquitous charge. I have behaved fair & straight with him in everything concerning the transaction. I can only think, that he is annoyed at my wanting to pay him off as he wanted his charges to run on.

The fact of the matter is the Sydney merchants think their clients belong to them body & soul, & I must say they generaly find a willing set of slaves.

I have now been in Sydney a week & have done nothing. I shall leave tomorrow night if I can. I went over & had dinner to day (Sunday) with Dr Badham. He & Mrs Badham desired to be remembered to you & my mother. I shall call on Sir James Martin before I go.

Your very affectionate son
Fred Trollope

The Lawyer I was telling you I saw is a man of the name of Slade. He dined [?] at Davis — the Barrister — one day when you & I where there.

Monday 17th

I thought I would try & see Smith himself this morning at the Bank of New South Wales & after spending two hours I was able to get him on the landing in the presence of another man. I explained to him my desire to pay off Watt & he refered me to the other manager. I suppose I will be able to pay off Watt through the agency of the Bank, but the affair is to them so small that they dont think it worth their attention.

I have just seen Jennings, & have explained to him that I should like to get into something larger as manager & part owner. He listened to me attentively, & said it was practicable. His own affairs were partnership affairs & they were sinking large sums of money to make them free hold. I asked him to let me know if he knew any such opening, & he promised in such a case to communicate with me. He was saying that this was a rather hard off time.

Sellers did not want to sell at reduced prices & buyers where hardly willing to pay the prices that had been ruling lately.

Smith was telling me that Bank interest was now 9 per cent.

Again I say good bye
Ever your affect: son
Fred Trollope

Most of the men Fred mentions in this letter were known to his father. Sir James Martin had been premier of New South Wales in 1871-72 and had been Anthony's host on a boat-trip down the Hawkesbury; he had also been present at a picnic in Anthony's honour at Warragamba, near Sydney, on 26 August 1875, during the novelist's second visit to Australia. Sir Patrick Jennings, another leading politician, had entertained Anthony at his Riverina property, Warbreccan, in July 1872. While Anthony was his guest, Jennings had nominated William Hay — the squatter with whom Fred discussed the "small place" on the Warrego that he had heard about — for the local seat of Murray: Anthony had made himself conspicuous at the nomination by vociferating his support for the cause of the free-selectors against the squatters. More recently, Jennings, Hay, and Anthony had appeared together on the platform at the O'Connell Centenary Celebration in Sydney on 6 August 1875.[17] Dr Badham, at whose home Fred had Sunday dinner, was Professor Charles Badham of Sydney University; Anthony refers to him in his *Australia and New Zealand* (Trollope's *Australia*, p. 230) as "prince of Professors and greatest of Grecians".

Fred did find a property; but to no avail. In the words of the obituary in the *Riverine Grazier*, he "purchased some back blocks near Cobar, but was prevented from working them, as for some years he had overtaxed his strength, and his health failed". The property near Cobar, known as Booroondara East, was presumably bought early in 1876; it was still on his hands, unsold and only partly paid for, when he wrote to his father from Inverell in January 1877. By this time he had obtained an appointment as an Inspector of Conditional Purchases in the Lands Department.

Letter 5   **Inverell**   **3 January 1877**

My dear Father
I have just got your letter of Oct. 18. It was sent to me by

Cramner [?] who had it sent him by the post office people by mistake.

By the same post Cramner [?] tells me that he is engaged to be married to Miss Robinson.

I half thought that would be the result of his stay in Sydney. She is certainly a handsome girl.

I have now got through nearly all the arrears of work left by Lord, (the inspector of this district) and I want to get permission to go to my own district. In the first place my staying here any longer is only wasting time, & secondly it is both uncomfortable & expensive to keep Susie in Sydney & be myself four hundred miles away.

But I cannot get a word of instruction from the land office people. Since I wrote you last we have had some frightful hot weather. I was for some days at a place called Bingara, & the combined influence of heat & dirt nearly killed me. I am not especialy dainty, but when the best diet one can get is sour bread & rotten eggs, one is apt to complain. The charge of this place exceeded that of the Australian Club. Their charge per diem for a horse was 16/- for oaten hay without corn. They never groom a horse, in fact they had neither brush or comb. I spent a very quiet Christmas day, but on the 29 of Dec: I found myself inspecting some selections belonging to a squatter named Gibson. He asked me to stay at his house till New Years day; which I did, & on that day he drove me over to a neighbouring station where there was some racing going on. So I had some small excitement.

I hear regularly from Susie. I dont think I could have left her in better quarters than where she is at present. She generally writes in good spirits and she says the children are jolly.

My chief trouble here is horses. Of course I have a great deal of riding to do, and besides having a good horse I must have a quiet one. The fellows up here ask such a tremendous price for a horse. You can hardly get an animal that will carry you for less than £20. A stranger wanting a horse is always run up. I was offered a good looking horse the other day in Warialda, they were asking £15 for him & offered me a trial. I rode him about forty miles & forty times he tried to break my neck. I need not say, no sale was made. I will now say a word about the Booroondara business — I got a telegram yesterday from the agent in Forbes, in whose hands it is for sale, that the drought prevented his buyer from going over there; so that it is not sold yet. Will you authorise Sir Hercules Robinson by letter to act as your Attorney in giving your consent to your becoming guarantor for the balance of the purchase money of Booroondara East. I will when I am in Sydney next go to the bank of N.S.W. & ask them if they will take up the bill with that security, of course they will at the same time hold the transfer of the block.

The bill becomes due on the 29th of June. As I have now got this appointment and am going to another part of the colony I shall still keep the place in the market, & if I can sell before that date of course I will not use your name. The block is so good that it will be worth a lot of money some day.

Give my love to Flo when you next see her; I have not written to her for a long time. She will forget all about me & I about her.

It is almost too late to wish you a merry Christmas & a happy new year, but I hope you have been jolly.

Your very affectionate son
Fred Trollope

Anthony Trollope's annotation on the back of this letter reads: "answered by letters to himself and Sir H. Robinson to back Fred's bill up to £750". The "Flo" to whom Fred sends his love was his mother's orphan niece Florence Bland, whom his parents had adopted in 1863 when she was still a child.

*   *   *   *   *

Fred's appointment in the Lands Department had been gazetted on 19 September 1876, and he was to remain in the department for the rest of his working life, retiring only a few months before his death. At the time he began his new career there he was twenty-nine and the father of three sons: Frank, Harry, and Frederic (Freddy). Notwithstanding his poor health most of his work had to be done on horseback, unprotected from the extremes of the colonial weather. Along with the folly and unfairness of his superiors in the Lands Department, the constant problem of making ends meet, and the difficulty of finding and keeping servants, the most frequently recurring topic in his letters during the next twelve years is the tortures that he and Susie suffered from the weather. Goulburn, his first posting, was too cold and after a few months he exchanged to Grafton. But Grafton, where he remained from 1877 to 1883, proved unbearably hot. Evacuation to the nearby beach at Clarence Heads every December or January afforded one means of relief from the heat, and the next letter in the University of Illinois collection was written just after such a "spell": by then Fred had been at Grafton for over three years.

Letter 6   Grafton   25 December [1880]

My dear Father
 I wish you a happy Christmas, although you will not get my letter until six weeks after.
 I got your letter of the 31 October a few days ago. You say that you are getting all very comfortable and jolly about your new house.[18] I can easily understand that money has to be spent getting every thing as you wish it. But as long as you do get things as you wish it, it is money well spent.
 We in a small way have had an overhaul of our house. Of course the Landlord did most of it for us.
 We have now had our spell at the Heads for a month, and were all glad to get home again.
 Susie and the children certainly are the better for it. I got leave of absence for three weeks, but as I was away from home for a month and in that time I did two weeks good work I consider I have only had a fortnights holiday. I thought that something would turn up to make it necessary for me to go to Sydney. But there is no especial reason for going at present, so I shall save my time and my money for a more urgent occasion.
 We do not forget your proposal about Frank going home.

He is going to school, and is learning something. He was delighted because he got a prize at the end of the last quarter.

Yes, I brought Nimrod home again after I lost him at Port Macquarie. Directly after I heard of him he was sent up to Kempsey. Having three horses of course I could not bring them all home, and so I left old Dick, as I had been riding him rather hard, on the Macleay, until the next trip. And there he is at present. It is a good thing to have a change horse so far from home. I shall pick him up as I go down the coast this time and leave one of the other horses behind in his place.

I shall have to go down to Port Stephen when I go down this time. My next trip is to New England. I start in about a weeks time. The 3 January is the time I have fixed. I shall then be away for about two months and shall have to go through the Glen Innes, Inverell, & Tenterfield districts. I think I had told you that they had given me two new districts — viz Inverell and Port Stephen. I thought I had as much as I could do before. Of course as I get to know the country well I can do the work quicker, but a country about as big as England and Scotland will take a good deal of knowing; or rather a good deal of riding over before you know it.

I like that chapter in Dr. Wortle's School, "Nobody has condemned you here."[19] It is the best in the book as far as I have read.

Susie sends a line by this post.

Your very affect: son
Fred Trollope

The proposal that Frank, Fred and Susie's eldest son (then aged eight), go to England to continue his schooling is pursued in later letters; and at least two trips to Sydney, in quest of a transfer ("removal") from Grafton, did subsequently eventuate. Fred's next letter, describing the first of them, indicates that his plan to set out for New England on 3 January must have been abandoned at the last minute: perhaps the narrow escape from an attack of "heat appoplexy", to which he refers in his opening paragraph, persuaded him that an immediate visit to Sydney was "necessary" after all.

Letter 7   Aarons' Exchange Hotel, Sydney   18 January 1881

My dear Father

I have come down to Sydney for a run to see if anything better is to be got than what I at present hold. My first shot was to call upon Sir John Robertson and explain to him that I was seeking a removal posting as Grafton did not agree with me or with any of us as far as climate is concerned — I do not know if I told you that about a fortnight ago I came home ill one night and had to send for the Dr. who told me that I had narrowly escaped having an attack of heat appoplexy — Sir John was in a "Scott" when I first saw him, and all I got from him was to be well sworn at. So that I cannot boast of much success in that line.

I then saw Plunket the Under Secretary for Justice, and he told me that he had my application for Police Magistrate and that he would keep it in memory, but that at present there were some others whose claims should be preferred to mine. That was a little better than Sir John.

I then went to see an old friend of mine Robert Wilkinson who has been for some time an M.P. for a squatting constituency. I told him what I was asking for and he promised that he would speak to the Minister for Justice who was a friend of his. So much for trying what interest will do.

In my own department the Chief and his sub expressed themselves as more than satisfied with my work. I find that I have now done more work than any other inspector and a great deal more than any other last year. I have two projects in hand, either to exchange with some officer in the country and get a better district or exchange with some officer in the Department in Sydney. I think Moriarty would like to have me in the office and if I could get an exchange for equal salary I would do it — That is £350. The advantage of the last is that there would be more chance of promotion. As an Inspector there seems to be no chance of promotion.

23 January, 81.

I now continue my letter commenced on 18th. I found I could not carry out the exchange in Sydney. So then came the question of the country exchange. I can get the Mudgee & Dubbo district & I took a run up to look at Dubbo where they want me to live. That I have made up my mind that I shall certainly not do. I want them to let me live in Bathurst where there are good schools and a good climate. But that they will not do. Then there is the alternative of Mudgee. I dare say you remember it near Gulgong. The climate is I think fairly good. But then there comes the question of a school.

There is the public school at all events and if there is nothing else it is not so far from Bathurst — Susie is so dead against Frank going home, at all events at present, as she says that she thinks she would never see him again. She thinks he would not live in England.

To go back to my own affairs. I think I shall shift to Mudgee. I shall not give them a decided answer until I go home and talk it over with Susie.

The objection is that living will be dearer; and keeping horses will be dearer. Last year I hardly made my travelling expenses pay the cost of travelling; but then my chief endeavour was to get as much work as possible done. The inspector who had the Mudgee district broke down more from hard work than from anything else.

There is a man in the Lands Office Russell by name who says that he was your fag at Harrow. I had a long yarn with him and he said that you once had a great fight and at last beat your man.

I was also talking of you to a man named Browne, at Dubbo. He is police magistrate there and seems a good fellow. He said that he met you at Gulgong. He scribbles a bit, and has written several passable stories, if not especially clever at all events honest; but he says that the publishers get every thing in the way of cash. But he said he intended to go on and quoted a saying of yours — "its dogged as does it" — and seemed to find some consolation in that.

My next letter will tell you what I have finally decided upon doing.

Your very affectionate son
Fred Trollope

When this letter was written Sir John Robertson, who had several times been Premier and Minister for Lands, was Vice President of the Executive Council. Robert Wilkinson, the "old friend" who promised Fred his good offices, was one of the members for Balranald in the

Legislative Assembly. "Moriarty" was A.O. Moriarty, Chief Commissioner of Conditional Sales in the Lands Office. The "man in the Lands Office" who had been Anthony Trollope's fag at Harrow was Henry Stuart Russell. Anthony also recalled the "great fight" at Harrow, proudly, in his *Autobiography* (pp. 13, 19). According to the *Harrow School Register, 1801-1893* (ed. R. Courtenay Welch) Russell had entered the civil service of New South Wales in 1866, though neither his appointment to the civil service nor his retirement from it appears to have been gazetted. In the early 1840s he had been one of the pioneers of the sheep-grazing industry in Queensland and a leading explorer. He had been a member of the New South Wales Legislative Council from 1853 to 1855 and had presumably joined the Lands Depàrtment after suffering financial reverses in 1866. His book *The Genesis of Queensland* was published in 1888, the year before his death in England.

The "man named Browne" who was police magistrate at Dubbo — and who was inspired to persevere with his "scribbling" by the saying of Giles Hoggett in Anthony Trollope's novel *The Last Chronicle of Barset*, "It's dogged as does it" — was of course Rolf Boldrewood, whose *Robbery under Arms* was serialized the following year. Fred had obviously not read one of the stories Boldrewood had already written, *The Miner's Right* (serialized in 1880). In this novel Anthony Trollope had been light-heartedly rebuked, under the name of "Anthony Towers", for his slighting remarks on Gulgong oratory in his *Australia and New Zealand*: Boldrewood himself had been one of the speakers at the public banquet given for Trollope at Gulgong in 1871.[20]

Whether because Susie was against moving to Mudgee or Fred himself had second thoughts, the family remained at Grafton.

Fred's next letter, written to his father from Grafton, is devoted exclusively to the proposal to send Frank home to England.

Letter 8 **Grafton** **10 October 1881**

My dear Father

I have now before me your letter of 11 August — all about Frank.

As to the boys powers — of course it is very hard to form a correct opinion. I have been talking to the master of his school. He says that Frank is as forward as a boy of his age generally is and that he ought to do well enough — so that evidently he forms no high opinion of his intellect. He — the master — says that Harry is sharper than Frank, but more idle — I should have thought it was just the other way on. But the greatest thing against Frank is that he is not strong. That shows itself in every way. It makes him talk carelessly, walk carelessly, & on days when he is not well do every thing the same way. It is easy to see that it comes from want of strength, and that if he keeps his health he will grow out of it. I believe his intellect to be better than Harry's, but Harry is more spry and ready. The moment Frank is tired he doesnt care. Harry doesnt tire so readily. Now comes the question is Frank fit to go to a more severe climate. From your last letter it appears that if he is to go he would have to go in the next twelve months — so as to be in England by the time he was ten years of age — or very soon after. No doubt he is gaining in strength but he is growing so fast that his strength [is] hardly in proportion to his age. Of course he goes to school every day — but he is not so good at taking his own part among his school fellows as Harry is. In England Frank would have to take his place at a preparatory boarding school in twelve months time or say eighteen months. I do not think that he would be strong enough for it. It would only be a waste of time and money to find out that and bring the boy back again, and I am afraid that would be the result. Of course I am not blind to the advantage that it would be to the boy to have the benefit of an English public school education. But his health must be the first consideration.

Would you be willing to do for Harry what you were promising to do for Frank.

As to my going to England — at present I see no hope.

My means of living would go. And it is not even as if I could come back and take up the same thing again.

I will get a copy of the register of the boys births so as to have them by me in case of necessity. Susie has another son. About this I write to my mother.

Your affect: son
Fred Trollope

Anthony wrote at the head of this letter: "answer saying that Harry is to be here before Easter 1883" (an instruction, presumably, to his niece Florence Bland, who frequently acted as his amanuensis during the last years of his life). However, by the time letter 12 was written, eleven months later, it had been decided that after all Frank, and not his younger brother, would run the gauntlet of an English public-school education.

The new son whose arrival Fred announces to his father — Arthur John — figures more prominently in his next letter.

Letter 9 **Grafton** 18[?] December 1881

My dear Mother

I have let a longer time go by without writing to you hoping to find that Susie had written. She wants me to tell you that having a young baby and no nurse for awhile she has had so very little time.

I am glad to say that upon coming back to Grafton I found Susie much better than when I went away. She is beginning to suffer a great deal from living in this climate. The Doctor here says that her liver is the cause of her suffering and that she must have a change.

I am now answering your letter of 4 October.

Thanks for the Blackwoods — I have today read the first part of "The Fixed Period." It is good fun.[21]

Thank you also for the photographs — they are very good.

We have just had a week of I think the most horrible weather I have ever suffered. Today a change came and we are all grateful.

I got through my work in the Richmond a little sooner than I expected. However I managed to do it all, & I have done the

1200 cases that I laid out to do at the beginning of the year. In fact I have done about sixty more than that number.

Jack is a very big fellow and promises to be strong and healthy.

We are going down to the Heads at the beginning of next month and Susie and the children will get some sea bathing to revive them for a bit.

There is no doubt that Grafton is a most trying climate. The heat is almost Indian, the atmosphere being very moist and dense.

Of course I get so much change that I do not feel it. But I do feel the constant travelling in hot weather, and being so much on horse back.

I am making an application for an appointment as Police Magistrate. There seems to be no chance of any promotion in my own department. When I came to Grafton I could live upon my salary more easily than I can now. We now have six children instead of three and the boys go to school. Then we could do with one servant and now we have two. I also have more work to do and consequently keep more horses and have to spend more money in travelling expenses in proportion to the salary I get. I should like to remain in the Lands Department, but as I said before there seems to be no prospect of promotion or increase of salary. I am not very hopeful of any immediate success from my application, but it can not do me any injury.

For the present good bye

Your very affect: son
Fred Trollope

Fred's application for appointment as a Police Magistrate was apparently no more successful than his previous one (Letter 7). His gazettal as an honorary magistrate back in 1872 — when his father had written to Henry Parkes on his behalf — doesn't seem to have counted as a qualification.

Susie had advertised for a "nurse-girl" in the *Clarence and Richmond Examiner* during April 1880 and was now without one again. In a later letter to his mother (Letter 12), Fred reported that Susie had been without a servant for three months; and by this time, as Fred points out in the letter above, they had six children.

The main topic of Fred's next letter, written to his father probably a few weeks later, is one that he never mentions to his mother: the plan for one of the elder boys to go to England. Less than three months before, he had proposed Harry, and Anthony had responded favourably; now it is clear that Fred has already changed his mind again and decided that Frank will probably be the lucky boy, though not for another year.

Letter 10 Clarence Heads 5 [January] 1882*

My dear Father

I have now been home something more than a fortnight from the Richmond and have been wanting to write to you ever since about Frank. I got the Doctor to examine him, and he says that the climate of the south of England would, he thinks, improve Franks constitution. But getting Susie to talk over the matter is like getting a dog to talk over getting a beating. She will only say that he is too young, and that when we first spoke of sending Frank home he was not to go until he was ten years old, and that now we are wanting to take him from her when he is only just nine. I thought after the Doctors recommendation she would look upon his going with more favor. But she will only say he is too young to go until he is ten years old. And as in the mean while the boy is getting on well at his school I dare say it is better to let him go for another twelve months.

Whenever he, or Harry, does go home I think they should land in England in the summer, as they have been living in such a very hot climate that they want to get into the cold weather by degrees. I fill up the paper you send me though in twelve months time of course there will be an alteration. I am

---

* The letter is dated "5 December '82", but given that it describes Frank (born 27 September 1872) as "only just nine", this must be a mistake. The fact that the family is now at Clarence Heads (cf. Letter 9) and that Fred is applying for leave of absence to go to Sydney (cf. Letter 11) suggests that Fred got the year right but the month wrong.

sorry to say that I do not make so much out of my work now as I did when I came to Grafton. I find now that when I pay for all I make nothing out of my travelling expenses. For I rarely stay any where except in Public houses, and I now have to work so fast that I get through my horses. Last year I nearly did as much work as I did in the first two years. I reported upon 1260 selections, and at the end I had more work in hand than I had at the beginning.

At the end of last month I sent in an application for an appointment as Police Magistrate. I am afraid that another years work at the same rate and in this climate would knock me up.

I came home the other day very unwell, and had to send for the Doctor. He said that I was done up and must do nothing for a fortnight and that I must not ride so much. All very well but what can one do. I now find that one of the commisionerships are vacant. I have made an application for leave of absence to go to Sydney and as soon as I get leave I will go and see if I can get promotion of some sort.

When I made my application for the appointment of Police Magistrate I wrote a private note to Sir John Robertson. He is now factotum. Parkes having gone to England and the Minister for Lands having resigned he is everything.[22] Those fellows in Sydney wont answer a telegram even for a week, and I cant leave until I get permission.

As you will see by the heading of my letter we are now at the Clarence river heads. Susie and the children can get some sea bathing and get out of that awful Grafton for a few weeks; for it has been terrible for the last few weeks. You would get up in the morning and find it sweltering. After a dull oppressive night you would have a blazing fierce day. Here it is fairly cool.

For the present good bye.

Your very affectionate son
Fred Trollope

Fred was granted the leave he had applied for: shipping lists in the *Clarence and Richmond Examiner* show that he sailed for Sydney on 11 January 1882 and arrived back in Grafton on 26 January.

Letter 11   **Sydney**   **24 January [1882]**

My dear Mother

I am sending you some photographs that I have had taken in Sydney this time. I dont think I have been taken since I was in Melbourne before I came home to England.[23] Susie made me promise that I would get done this time. I felt very much inclined to get out of it, as going to the photographer is next thing to going to the Dentist.

I am afraid that is the only result of my trip to Sydney. As far as I can see there is no hope of any promotion. However if anything turns up I have a better chance of getting it from having asked. Susie is, as you know, at the Clarence heads. Her sister Nellie is with her.

Old Bolding and I have now parted company. I am sorry for it — for though he was the most prosy man I ever came across, still he was a gentleman, and a good man. Blythe is hardly a gentleman, is certainly not a good man but is very clever, and is very witty and amusing.

He is certainly a better commissioner than Bolding for he grasps the facts of a case at once, whereas Bolding meanders round it and never seems to touch it. On the other hand Bolding works much harder than Blythe.

I was hoping that I should be able to effect an exchange with one of the men in the office in Sydney. The head of our office would have liked it, but the man did not care to make the exchange. There would have been more prospect of promotion inside the Sydney office than there is in the country.

Sydney has certainly improved since I was here last.

Some of the new Government buildings and warehouses are very good.

Melbourne is doing herself so much harm with her protection policy that Sydney finds her opportunity in Melbourne's folly. At the same time Melbourne is geographically so much better situated that I believe she will always be the principal town. Then Victoria has the advantage of a better climate.

My love to Flo. I hope she is now well again.

                                    Your very affectionate son
                                    Fred Trollope

When Fred's next letter in the Illinois collection was written it was midwinter, but his preoccupation with the weather is as strongly in evidence as usual. The distaste which the letter expresses for the piety of the Manning River settlers would have pleased his father, who inherited a hearty detestation of evangelicals from his mother.

Letter 12 **Taree, Manning River** **19 July 1882**

My dear Mother

    I am again as you will see by the heading of my letter "on the wallaby" — and what is worse I am having bad weather for it; however that must be taken the bad with the good. On the whole I would sooner travel in the winter taking the occasional spells of bad weather than in the summer, and suffer the heat. For the heat of the Clarence and Richmond in the summer is very trying.

    I generally manage to get a trip to New England every summer and that always does me good, but poor Susie has not that advantage and the bad climate of Grafton has told upon her. Her great trouble is servants. The good one that we had for twelve months left us about a month ago, and now she has none at all and the work is making her ill. I dare say she has written to you about her complaint. I shall have to take her away from Grafton for a change in the summer.

    When I left home the boys were very well. Freddy in particular is strong and growing well.

    Fanny is fat and jolly, but poor little Effie is often ailing.

                                     26 July 82

    I now finish the letter I began a week ago. As I was afraid the new Commissioner for the district has just fixed his courts as I did not want him to — I have been scrambling to get through my work, and have been at it long hours. I thought I would finish this district before the Commissioner came as he only is holding court at Port Macquarie and that is sixty miles on my way home towards Graton.

    But I am sorry to say that I can't get through and so shall have to come back again to the Manning from Port Macquarie.

    I have given myself a severe cold by being a good deal out in the wet, and being out late in the evenings.

We have had some really cold weather lately reminding me of an English November.

I shall not be more than a week at home after this trip before I have to go up to New England as Blythe is holding a court up there at which I shall have to attend. They are a great church going lot on the Manning river in fact it is their favourite amusement. Dancing and singing they think ungodly. They are strong in protestant halls, young mens Christian associations, and temperance societies. Chief among the elect are the storekeepers. They quarrel among themselves and back bite each other pretty extensively, but that I suppose is to prevent them from being too good.

Good bye for the present.

Your very affectionate son
Fred Trollope

The two girls, Frances Kathleen (Fanny) and Effie Madeleine, had been born in 1878 and 1879. In Fred's next letter he promises to send his mother a photo of Fanny. He also defends the name Jack, which his mother perhaps considered a little demotic.

Letter 13   **Grafton**   **3 September 1882**

My dear Mother

I have now your letter of 4 June 82. Thanks for the Photos of the house. We will get Fanny photographed and send one to you. As you say Babies are just as much alike as peas and their characteristics are not much more developed. Did I not send you a brigand. If I have one I will send it only you will at once go and lock up all your spoons.

Poor Susie has now been without a servant for three months. She certainly has a nurse girl who helps her a good deal. If the hot weather comes and finds her without, it will lay her up. In fact she is unwell at present. The Doctor says that I shall have to take her away this summer.

The farming community are so well off here that they do not care to send their daughters out to service. This is a state of things that any right minded person would rejoice at. I am, on this occasion, not right minded.

I send you one packet of the seeds you spoke of. "The Desert Pea" I have asked two or three people that had it growing to save me some, and probably I may get it, "some day".

So I have given your list to a nursery man telling him also to send any particularly good Australian flowers that he can get me the seeds of. They will come anon. I began gardening when I came here — but the combined efforts of couch grass, and writing reports, has been too much for gardening.

Why dont you like the name of Jack? I think it is the grandest name out. I dont know how the present baby got to be called Jack. There was no discussion about it. He was called Jack half an hour after he was born & it has never been anything but Jack since.

Good bye.

Give my love to all at home, including Mary Davis if she is still with you. Susie sends her love.

Your very affect son
Fred Trollope

P.S. The Brigands is out, they is.

F.T.

Mary Davies had been a friend of Fred's mother since just after her marriage; Mrs Trollope had given a dinner party for her just before she wrote to Fred on 4 June.[24] The "Brigands", twice mentioned in Fred's letter, presumably belong to some family game. Surprisingly the letter makes no reference to the revived plan for young Frank to go to England for his schooling: this seems to have been regarded as a matter for the men to settle on their own.

Letter 14   Grafton   5 September 1882

My dear Father

You see that I am home again, though it is not to be for a very long time. I am off for New England in a few days time. About the £30 cheque, when you sent it you said that I was to destroy it if I did not use it to pay for Franks passage and I did destroy it.

I wrote you a few days ago about sending one of the boys

home. If I do not hear from you saying that he cannot go, I will send Frank about the end of March next.

I suppose that the Orient line is the best.

About the names and dates of the youngest of the children.

Effie Madeleine was born on the 29 December 1879 and as she was baptized by a scotch parson she has no god father or mother except myself & Susie as her parents.

Jack was baptized in the Church of England his sponsors are Susie and myself. He was born upon the 30 September 1881, and his name is Arthur John. But he is and will be *Jack*.

He is like nobody else in the world if he is not like you, and he is so far a great deal bigger and stronger than any of the other children, & if this beastly climate of Grafton does not injure him he will be a big fellow.

I was not surprised to hear of your being in Ireland when I got Flo's letter, as I saw by the papers that you were there. What an everlasting trouble those Irish fellows are. Let them ask for whatever they like and if they can show reason and justice for what they ask I believe they will eventually get it — down to Home Rule. I mean Home Rule in the same way as the state of New York has Home Rule. But if they go in for independence, they must be crushed, if necessarily, utterly. But nothing should be conceded to them except by reason.

They should be taught that they cannot work upon our fears. I must say that I think the letting those men out of jail in the hopes that they would use their influence with the Irish was an unEnglish thing to do.[25] They take a long time to draw up poor Arabi. Of course it has to be done but it is unsatisfactory work.[26]

But all these are trifles. The only one real burning question for the world is — Will they make a railway from Grafton into the interior?[27] All questions of race, crede, science, etc, pale before this.

Give my love to Flo and ask her to write on her own account.

Your very affectionate son
Fred Trollope

Anthony presumably required the information about the three younger children for Debrett's Peerage (in which he and his family figured as distant relatives of a baronet). His visit to Ireland was to gather material for his last (and unfinished) novel *The Landleaguers*, in which he announced that he was ending his lifelong adherence to the Liberal party because of its Irish policy: like Fred he believed that it was "necessary, — necessary at any rate for England's safety, — that Ireland should belong to her" (*The Landleaguers*, 1883, 3, p. 148).

Fred's letter of 5 September 1882 is his last to his father in the Illinois collection. Anthony suffered a stroke on 3 November 1882 and died just over a month later, on 5 December. Fred would no doubt have received news of his stroke and subsequent death by telegraph and have written to his mother in response to the news; but in the Illinois letters his only reference to Anthony's death occurs in one written over two months after the event, and there it is overshadowed by a momentous piece of news of his own: escape from the "beastly climate" of Grafton had finally been achieved.

Letter 15   [Sydney]   **18 February 1883**

My dear Mother

I have now just got Harrys letter of December. Of course before I got his letter I knew what it contained. He told me of our dear Fathers death.

I was so glad to hear that he did not suffer much pain during his illness.

I must send you a few lines that have been written in a Sydney paper.[28] I do not know the writer but I hope I shall some day.

I have also had some very kind letters from some of my friends about my father. I must send you one or two of them some day.

...* you that I brought Susie to Sydney some little time ago.

I intended only to stay a few days and leave her here — but the day before I intended going Mr. Moriarty the head of our

---

* I am unable to decipher several words at this point.

department asked me if I would like to stay and do some office work. He then said that there was nobody in the office who had any knowledge of the field work, and asked me if I would accept a clerkship at £400 per annum. He is trying to get it put on the estimates for the year, and if it is put on I shall have the first offer of it. I should have had the first vacant commissionership — and one of them died the other day, but another of the inspectors got it. He was the first inspector appointed and therefore my senior. But I still think they should have given it to me, as I have done so much more work than any other inspector.

I was a good two years work ahead of any other Inspector, though the man who got the appointment had quite two years work the start of me. This last year I did more than twice as much work as anybody else. I have not decided to take the Sydney appointment. The fact is that it is hard enough to live in Grafton on £350 a year and there I am away nearly always. Sydney is much more expensive and I shall be always at home.

In Grafton though we dont live grandly we are very comfortable. We have a good house and a good school for the boys.

Now in Sydney rents are most exorbitant, you cant get a house under a hundred a year, and that is not much of a place.

The servants wages are frightful. 15/- a week for general servants. And 10/- a week for nurse girls. No doubt the Colony is prosperous and business people are making fortunes, but then I am not a business person. On the other hand I think in Sydney I have more chance of promotion. At present I stand as well in the eyes of the heads of the Department as I can do. Whether I should do so having daily contact with them I cannot say.

Then Susie has had bad health at Grafton. And though this change seems to be doing her good, and she will not in any case go back to Grafton until the hot weather is over still I should like for her sake to remove. There will probably be a vacancy among the Commissioners again before

[Incomplete]

The shipping list in the *Clarence and Richmond Examiner* for 30 January 1883 shows that Fred, Susie, three of the children, and a servant had sailed from Grafton on the *Helen Nicoll* on 24 January. Presumably it had been intended that Susie would remain in Sydney with the children to await the birth of her seventh child (Clive).

* * * * *

Fred's subsequent career seems to bear out his fear that proximity might not improve his relations with his official superiors. It also confirms the surprising hint — in his remark "though we dont live grandly we are very comfortable" — that distance might lend enchantment even to Grafton. But, notwithstanding his doubts, he did accept the clerkship in Sydney. According to the obituary notice in the *Riverine Grazier*, his position was in effect that of Chief Inspector though "no such appointment was ever formally made".

Letter 16   Lands Department (Sydney)   19[?] July 1883

My dear Mother
Having overtaken all my work I write you from the Office. The Land office is in a cronic state of nerves [?]. I can see no reason why it should be so, but men idle their time away so dreadfully and the men who are willing to work are left with more than their proper share. As my work is special, in advising what course should be taken in each case that the inspectors report upon, and I have to do all of that class of work, nobody else can throw their work upon me, only it does not come through to me as quickly as it should do. It is dreadful to see some of the men, they take out the newspaper, they talk and yarn, and do a hundred and fifty things, while the work is urgently pressing, and then they call out that more men are wanted; until at last the clerks are in each others road.
I have now got your letter of the 31st May. Thank you for the money. I have sent the cheque home for collection as they charge so much for discount.
What a good thing Harry did not make up his mind to meet

Frank in Plymouth. I mean on account of the railway accident.

I intended delaying sending, or rather writing, this letter hoping to hear of Frank's arrival before I again wrote. But I now write without waiting longer.

The dear old boy wrote us from Suez, and he then seemed happy and contented, and said that the other passengers had been good to him.

I think I told you before he [?] started that I gave the stewardess a good tip to look after his clothes.

I shall be sorry to hear of your leaving Harting. When Harry gets married it would be surely not more expensive living at Harting, than breaking up the house and going to a new house. Of course you know best. I only say I shall be sorry if it is done. It is so hard to get a place that you like. We are very comfortable in our little house.

The situation is healthy and there is plenty of room out of doors for the children to run about. It has been a little dull for Susie, not having a friend near her; but on the whole we [?] might have very easily have done worse. I think that rents are falling in Sydney. For the last few years they have been abnormally high. Where on earth all the people came from who paid the rents I do not know. But trades people have been making great profits the last few years. Goods have come from the manufacturer at a low rate and they have been retailed at high rates by the shopkeepers. Sydney has undergone a great alteration since you were here. I do not mean socially, as really I do not know. But then the huge wharehouses and banks where before there were only

[Incomplete]

The "railway accident" which Fred's brother Harry providentially avoided by deciding not to meet Frank at Plymouth was probably one that occurred near Clapham Junction on 27 June 1883 and was reported in the following day's *Times* under the headline "Fatal Accident on the London and South-Western Railway". Harry's impending marriage, referred to in the letter, took place the following year.

The letter is the first of many in which Fred acknowledges receipt of money from his mother. Under his father's will nothing would come to him until after the death of his mother — who in the event outlived him by several years. His patrimony was the £6,000-odd that had been sunk in his sheep stations. Acknowledging a cheque for £50 from his mother in a later letter (19), he exclaims ruefully, "I feel like a cormorant eating you up". On another occasion (Letter 20) he gives his consent, as required under the terms of his father's will, to his mother's selling a parcel of shares; but he does so reluctantly because he fears that the sale may "make a hole" in her income — which Anthony had intended to be sufficient to sustain the same "way of living" as she enjoyed before his death. No doubt his mother was moved by his constant complaints about the expensiveness of Sydney, but in any case she would probably have felt it only fair that he should have access to at least some of the wealth (£26,000) which his father had amassed, and of which Fred would presumably inherit a half-share eventually. She knew, at any rate, that however squeezed he may have been for money, part of what she sent him was devoted to the purchase of land (or perhaps further land) on the Richmond river. By 6 July 1884 (Letter 21) he had three small properties there worth about £500, though he at that time received no rent for them. Six years later (Letter 25) he also mentions a property on the Macleay river; but because of bad seasons this has returned him no rent since he bought it nearly a year ago, and he wishes he had held on to his mining shares — though he got a good price for them. By 1890 he was on a considerably higher salary and was back in inexpensive Grafton, but even when he was battling with Sydney's high cost of living in 1883-84 his financial position can hardly have been as difficult as he was inclined to paint it to his mother — and no doubt to himself.

Before Fred had been a year in Sydney a new bill, designed "to decentralize the land department", was introduced in the New South Wales parliament. Fred mentions it almost casually in his letter to his mother of 14

October 1883, clearly not anticipating how profoundly and how "detrimentally" it might affect his future life.

Letter 17   **Sydney**   **14 October 1883**

My dear Mother

We have now got your letters of the 10th and 16 July, also of the 26 August. Being away from home I have of course been getting your letters irregularly and consequently have been irregular in answering them. I have now got the box, that is I mean seen the contents. Thanks for sending every thing. I think every thing will be of use except the black waistcoats. The boots are a little big but not uncomfortable. The coats fit me first rate. I shall only have to have the buttons put a little further back, that is all. The trowsers I shall have to take to a Tailor. If I can only come across a man who will take trouble I shall be well fitted out for the next twelve months.

We were very glad to hear such a good account of Frank's health. I only hope that his schoolmaster will really make him knuckle down to work. Frank can work very well and is smart enough but he has to be told that he must do it, or else look out for squalls.

I shall not be altogether done out of my increase as I thought at one time that I should be. For the time I am in Sydney I am to get an allowance for the purpose of keeping my travelling equipment up.

For next year it is hard to say what may be done. A new land bill is before the house, and if it passes there will be a great change in the department. The present idea is to decentralize the land department of the colony, and to do so by putting the responsibility into the hands of country boards. I suppose that it will in some way affect my position but I cannot think that any change will be detrimental to me. Of course there will still be Inspectors but I fancy they will have more Inspectors and that they will have a smaller sallary. But the bill will have to be passed first and there is likely to be a fierce debate over it.

I am sorry to say that financially we are getting bad news from England, failures and money getting tight. Business people in Sydney are beginning to find that things are not so rosy as they were last year and the year before, and consequently our . . .* tells the tail. At present we are not of the highest taxed people in the world, but I expect we shall find that we shall before long have to bear the cost of government. Our debt is nothing for it has been nearly all expended in railways which rather more than pay the interest. But here people expect the government to do everything. Education alone is an enormous item being over £600,000 and fast increasing. Then our post and Telegraph offices are still being worked at a loss.

Good bye dear Mother. I hope you are in good health. We send letters to Frank by this mail. Susie writes so that I have to give no message from her.

Your very affect son
Fred Trollope

It is clear from this and from Fred's next letter that his expectation that he would be "always at home" while in Sydney had not been realized. Presumably he was already acting as a Commissioner of Conditional Purchases under the 1875 Lands Act, though his appointment as such, on a temporary basis, was not gazetted till 1 May 1884. His next letter complains bitterly of the tedium, expense, and futility of the travelling which his new appointment demanded. But both it and the two that followed it — in quick succession — make it equally clear that Sydney itself had sadly disappointed him.

Letter 18 Clavering Cottage, Enfield [Sydney] 6 January 1884

My dear Mother

I am now answering your letter of the 28 October. I have for the last five weeks been away from home attending those wretched courts of Inquiry. I have asked the heads of the office not again to subject me to the awful infliction that it is — to say nothing about the tremendous waste of time.

I have as I said before been five weeks away, and my salary with travelling expenses in that time will cost £75. And yet the

---

* I am unable to decipher a word here.

work done has been nothing. However when the new Act is passed, there will be some alteration.

I am sorry to say when I came home I did not find matters looking well. Susie is far from well and I had to get the Doctor to come and see her at once. She has been worried by having the children all more or less ailing. Freddy, who used to be such a sturdy little fellow has a weak chest. Even Fanny is getting thin. I am writing to you in one of those detestable days that we get in this climate. Every thing is hot and muggy and every body is more or less cross.

I have been just reading the notice of my Fathers Autobiography in the Times.[29] If I could not write a better notice than that I should not write one at all. I do not mean because it is not sufficiently favourable, but because it is colourless. There is scarcely an expression of opinion in it. It is written by one of your conventional men without a soul of his own. However as far as it goes it is a favourable review. I'll lay five to two that the man who wrote it never put his bones outside a horse. You might have told our father that he was a bad official — That he did not understand the first principles of novel writing, and he might have ignored that slander, but to say that he hunted but never saw the hounds — "What is truth, spake jesting Pilate"!

I do think the Autobiography is a most charming piece of writing. I do not think that the Prime Minister is either the best or the second best of his novels.[30] The Times critic is true when he says that he was constantly recovering himself and after one or two poorer novels a good one would succeed.

But I do think that period which followed his going to Waltham was his best and that Orley Farm was not only the best but decidedly the best of all his novels.[31]

It troubles Susie that Frank speaks badly. He certainly was better than that when he was at home. I only hope that his schoolmaster will be properly severe with him. I am glad that he writes to you constantly. As you say he can learn but is very idle. Anything that interests him he learns fast enough. Harry is getting on fairly well. He has a good memory.

Your affect: son
Fred Trollope

Letter 19 **Clavering Cottage** **16 January 1884**

My dear Mother

I have duly got your letter enclosing the draft for £50. I feel like a cormorant eating you up, as if I shouldn't be drawing upon your income. Thank you for the money.

I some times feel sorry I left Grafton. For there we were comfortably off. Things being cheaper than they are in Sydney. Then I have been put out of my calculations as to income by the way in which the Lands people reneged upon me about the arrangement that was made at the beginning of last year. I then distinctly understood that I was to get £75 per annum increase so long as I chose to remain in Sydney doing special work. The best arrangement I have been able to make was to have an advance at that rate paid me while I was in Sydney, which advance was to cease when I left Sydney for the country.

For last year I got from them about £40 which was consumed in keeping my equipment, horses, etc, while I was in Sydney. I was then promised that an amount of £100 per annum was to be put on to my salary for the ensuing year. That has not been done as they would not make any increase pending a change in the land bill.

I can now only hope that when the change does come I may find that things work to my benefit. I do not want to bother you with my complaint but I do wish I could do without drawing upon your income.

I got the photograph of our Fathers grave by the same mail. The cardboard was altogether broken, so I am having the photograph taken off and framed. When I last wrote you Susie was very unwell. I am glad to say she is better now.

We have been having some frightful weather. 105 in the shade in Sydney. The country is suffering very much from drought. In places all the stock are dying.

Give my love to Flo

Your very affect. son
Fred Trollope

Letter 20   Clavering Cottage, Enfield   20 January 1884

My dear Mother

I am now replying to your letter of the 25 November 83 in which you speak of selling out 55 shares in the Standard Bank of South Africa.

I send my reply by the same post as a letter I wrote a few days ago, and which I have been keeping for a while.

Again thank you for the £50 which has safely come to hand. I do not find that there has been any charge. It should indeed be the other way. You should be able to purchase the draft at a small premium — I hope it has not been any trouble doing this — And so my dear mother as to your proposition of selling out the Standard shares.

Of course Jones advice will go with you a long way. It seems to me that you are getting a very good interest for the money. But I am not in a position to judge if the sale is advisable or not. 55 shares at £45 would realize £2475 and £164 per annum is nearly 7 per cent. I give my consent on a separate sheet as you may wish to keep the scrap of paper by you. But [don't] my dear Mother let us make too big a hole in your income. I know it was our fathers desire to let his death make no difference in your way of living as far as money matters went.

I like the photo of our Fathers grave and stone. It seems to be handsome and massive.

I have had the photo framed in an ebony . . .* frame.

If I remain in Sydney I shall have to get a bigger house. We like the place we are in very well and have plenty of ground, but the house is not big enough for us. Our dining room is 15ft by 12. Then seven of us have to sit down to table. The drawing room is the same size and the three bed rooms are smaller, then there is a kitchen & girls room and a pantry. Our great luxury is that we have plenty of land — about an acre. For this we have to pay £72 per annum. Then we are a mile and a half away from the nearest railway station, and that is the 9th station from Sydney. By being very sharp, I can, if the trains are punctual, get to the office in just an hour. But it always takes me more than an hour coming out.

---

* I cannot decipher a word here.

Susie had such a nice letter from Mr Robinson telling her all about Frank. I am sorry to hear that he is a sloven. Of course at home he had more done for him than he could have at school, but I am afraid he exhibited such tendencies always. I do hope he will be rigorously kept to his work, and that he will not allow the money spent on his education to be wasted. I know that Frank can do well if he chooses. We made excuses for him when in Grafton for the enervating climate of the Clarence made him languid. We have had a terrible burst of hot weather. I am glad that we were away from Grafton. There they have had it 105 in the shade for a week.

Your very affect son
Fred Trollope

The home in which Fred and his family had lived so comfortably in Grafton had been in Maud Street: Susie had given this address when advertising for servants in the *Clarence and Richmond Examiner*, and it also appears in contemporary editions of Debrett's Peerage. Clavering Cottage, Enfield, where his three letters to his mother in January 1884 were written, was to remain the family residence, off and on, until Fred died in 1910. With five children old enough to sit down to table with their parents, and a sixth in the nursery, it is not surprising the family felt cramped; one assumes that at some later stage the landlord was induced to enlarge the house. It was situated just off Liverpool Road, in a suburb then known as either Enfield or Redmyre, later as Strathfield, and later again as Summer Hill. By the early 1900s the Post Office Directory gave its address as the corner of Henson Street and Junction Road, Summer Hill.

Within a year of writing Letters 18-20 (above), Fred was to face worse heat than that of Sydney and, as he was soon to decide, very much worse than that of Grafton; but when he next wrote to his mother he was obviously unaware of the fate that the "new Act", the 1884 Land Bill, held in store for him. His next two letters are from Corowa, to which his duties as temporary Commissioner of Conditional Purchases (under the old land act) had briefly taken him.

Letter 21 **Corowa** **6 July 1884**

My dear Mother

Forgive my writing on this beastly paper but travelling one sometimes gets stuck up. I have just got your letter of 15th May. I first of all attend to your request to send a duplicate letter of sanction re the Standard Bank Shares. Thank you for the £50. I have no doubt that I shall hear all about it on my return to Sydney a week hence.

But you are sending me more than the proposed amount. Any money that I have more than what I want for my immediate necessities — and it is not much — I put it in to the purchase of land on the Richmond River. I own three small properties there now, worth about £500. I get no rent from them but that is about their selling value.

I am at present at a small town on the Murray River just below Albury. It is close to where the Grays live. In fact I have had several of their cases to inquire into, and have in this way met John Gray. He is a good fellow.

The other brother George Gray has gone home to England. I think George made an unfortunate marriage. I remember when I first came to Australia having a letter to them from the Millais, which I sent to them by post, writing myself at the same time. They never in any way acknowledged my letter, so of course I heard no more about them.

The police magistrate at Corowa is Reginald Hare. He was at school with my father at Winchester. He is a son of Francis George Hare, whome I never heard of till now, and a nephew of Julius Hare whome I have read of in Forsters life of W. Savage Landor.

Hare the P.M. here is a good prosy old fellow. He has been most kind to me.

I am indeed glad to get such a good account of Frank, and I hope that he will repay the care that has been taken of him. I do not think that he is an ungrateful boy.

Good bye my dear Mother. Your ever affect: son
Fred Trollope

Letter 22   **Corowa**   **7 July 1884**

My dear Mother
   Since I wrote yesterday your letter of the 18th May has been forwarded to me enclosing a bill of Lading for "one package of merchandise" and a Draft in the form of a letter to "Comptoir d'Escompte de Paris," from the Union Bank of London for £50.
   I shall be in Sydney next Monday — that is this day week.
   I have no doubt that when I get there I shall find the box as right as the money.
   In the meanwhile I answer your letter the moment I get it.
   As I wrote at length yesterday I need say no more.
   Good bye dear Mother. Thank you for the Books and the money.
                              Ever your own affect son
                              Fred Trollope

The Reginald Hare who was Police Magistrate at Corowa was the younger brother of G.E.C. Hare, whom Anthony Trollope had met in 1872 at Albany, Western Australia (where Hare was Resident Magistrate) and whom he had also known at Winchester.[32] Both Francis Hare and his brother Julius were intimate friends of Walter Savage Landor and are mentioned frequently in John Forster's *Life* of Landor (1869). Reginald was in fact the half-brother of Francis and Julius, not (as Fred states) the son of Francis. John and George Gray were brothers of Effie Gray, who married John Ruskin and subsequently, after that marriage was annulled, the painter J.E. Millais; Millais illustrated some of Anthony Trollope's novels and became his close friend. George Gray went to Australia in 1856 to farm sheep but did not prosper and returned to England after ten years. He died unmarried in 1924, at the age of ninety-five. The other brother, John Gray, apparently stayed permanently in Australia.[33]

* * * * *

The changes that the year 1883 produced in Fred Trollope's life — his transfer to Sydney and the departure of his eldest son to England — were as nothing compared to those which occurred the following year. Ostensibly the 1884 Lands Act brought him promotion — increased responsibility and a higher salary (£650 per year) — but it also took him for two and a half years to Wilcannia, where he was separated from his wife and children (who remained in Sydney) and subjected to such infernal discomforts that even Grafton quickly came to appear almost a paradise in comparison.

Fred arrived to take up his appointment as Chairman of the Local Land Board for the Land District of Wilcannia on 3 February 1885. His appointment had been gazetted over a month earlier and the *Wilcannia Times*, which had announced it as early as 22 December 1884, had long since become fretful over his non-arrival. The *Times* also recalled, however, that Fred had presided over a land court in Wilcannia several months before. This prior acquaintance with the town perhaps explains why he was in no hurry to take up his duties.

Not surprisingly, his two letters from Wilcannia — one to his mother and the other to his brother Harry — are the most desolate, and the most wistfully affectionate ("My own Dearest Mother", "My Dear old Harry"), of all the letters in the Illinois collection.

Letter 23   Wilcannia   16 May 1886

My own Dearest Mother

I have intended writing to you every day since I got your last letter but when I got clear of my office work I have been so sick of writing that I have kept putting it off from day to day.

I used to have two clerks here, but at the beginning of this year when I came back from Sydney there was so little work doing, the chief clerk in particular being altogether unemployed, that I recommended his removal, and now though we have not more work than we can get through, yet we have quite sufficient to keep two men employed. I am supposed to have the services of another clerk when I require them, those of the Crown Lands Agent; whose own work only keeps him going a few hours a day. However he is not much use to me as he always has more urgent business of his own to attend to when I want his services. So consequently I amuse him occasionally by keeping him in after office hours. But I have one excellent clerk.

I have now got to hate Wilcannia most horribly. First of all living away from Susie and the children is uncomfortable and expensive. Though I have a larger salary as Chairman of the Land Board than I had as Commissioner, yet I find I am considerably worse off. The home expenses are of course just the same as if I was at home. Then my board here costs me £2 per week — I certainly do not get much for that as I sleep in a room that you cannot keep a candle alight in on windy nights and the less I say about our diet the better. I cannot regret that I did not bring Susie and the children here. About a month ago some teams arrived from Bourke with flour, for three weeks prior to that we had been living on weevils which had been living on flour. Every thing is bad and every thing is dear. And a worse place for children I cannot immagin.

I shall hang on until the end of this year and then I shall make a frantic appeal to the powers that be for a removal.

I must try and get time to write Frank by this mail. Give my love to Flo.

Your very affectionate son
Fred Trollope

Contemporary numbers of the *Wilcannia Times* are full of references to the appalling summer heat, sand drifts, and lack of civilized amenities. But Fred's next letter, written to his brother at the beginning of 1887, makes no reference to his "frantic appeal" for a removal; on the contrary, it states that he saw no immediate prospect of escape from Wilcannia. It was presumably written mainly to congratulate Harry on the birth of his daughter Muriel, but its first paragraphs deal with his own dismal plight.

Letter 24   **Wilcannia**   **2 January [1887]***

My Dear old Harry

I got your letter of the 16 November a few days ago.

As you will see by the heading of my letter I am still in Wilcannia, and of course I hate the place more than ever, and God only knows when I will get away from the place. In the mean while Susie has two of the children ill with scarlett fever. I believe however that they are doing very well, or as well as can be expected. But the anxiety makes her ill.

Every body tells me that I have got to look very old since I came to Wilcannia. It is certainly one of those cursed places that no man of over 30 years of age ought to be sent to.

I am glad to get a good account of Ada and the Bairn. I often think how much better it is for you to have a wife and child than to remain a solitary old Batchelor.

Of course Muriel will be awfully spoilt, but then spoiling does girls no harm. I only hope that Frank will not get spoilt. Spoiling does boys a great deal of harm. My Mother made me unhappy by telling me how idle Frank was. I hope he will have that knocked out of him. He must be taught to work and he cannot begin too young.

So you are going to publish a novel. I am sorry to hear Ada say that it is dull.[34] In any case I wish you every luck with it.

I am very glad to hear that Uncle Tom has got a pension but what has he done for his pension.[35]

You say that you have taken to smoking again. I never knew that you had knocked off. Do you remember when you rode up from Bathurst to Mortray you were only to put up a few things in a valise, and by way of keeping down the impedementa you only put in "fourteen" pipes.

Good bye old fellow and love to Ada and Muriel.

By the way you have your wish. Lord Randolph Churchill has apparently snuffed himself out for the present.

I do hope that Hartington will join with Salisbury. But I am afraid that a feeling of mistaken loyalty to the old party will prevent it.

---

* The letter is dated "2 January 1886", but its references to British politics indicate that it was in fact written at the beginning of 1887.

I should like to see you fellows in England give France a dig — jump on her stomach in fact.

Your very affectionate brother
Fred Trollope

Fred's remarks on English politics here confirm that both he and his brother had become Tory in their sympathies (though Fred's last letter home — Letter 26 — indicates that he never lost his faith in the basic Liberal doctrine of free trade, a faith that was proclaimed also in Letter 11). Lord Randolph Churchill, the youngest chancellor of the exchequer since Pitt, resigned from Salisbury's Conservative ministry at the end of 1886, after only four months in office. Salisbury had offered Lord Hartington, whose Liberal Unionists held the balance of power in parliament after the 1886 election, the prime ministership in a coalition government of Conservatives and Liberal Unionists; Hartington declined, but he did later defect to the Conservatives.

Fred's appeal for a removal from Wilcannia apparently succeeded more thoroughly than he had expected, for by August 1887 the town had lost not only him but its status as "headquarters" of a land district. Though a new land court building had been erected in the town as recently as August 1885, the Lands Department announced the transfer of the Wilcannia land board to the jurisdiction of the Bourke board at the beginning of August 1887. Later the same month Fred's appointment as a temporary member of the Local Land Board for the District of Deniliquin was gazetted, and a year and two days later (on 28 August 1888) his appointment as Acting Chairman of the Local Land Boards for the Land Districts of Grafton, Casino, Kempsey, Lismore, and Murwillumbah. After more than three years in the backblocks, separated from his family, he clearly returned to Grafton with relief.

* * * * *

Grafton was apparently as pleased at his return as was Fred himself. The *Clarence and Richmond Examiner* — in the same issue as that in which it reported his arrival by the *City of Grafton* (18 August 1888) — ran a story headed "Changes in the Local Lands Office" which reveals that Fred's appointment followed a lengthy inquiry by a Lands Board Commission into the working of the Local Lands Board office under its previous chairman; the inquiry had reported unfavourably on Fred's predecessor who, as a result, had been recalled to Sydney along with his son ("who has hitherto occupied the position of clerk in the office over which his father presided"). The *Examiner* noted that the new chairman had "formerly occupied an important official position in this district in connection with the Lands department" and saw every reason to hope that the Board would deal with cases more expeditiously and meet more regularly under the "new *régime*". A few weeks later, on 8 September, the paper commented on the "large amount of business" the board had transacted during a six-day sitting just completed, a sitting over which Mr Trollope had presided throughout, showing himself to be "a capable officer for the position". Susie and the children — of whom the last, Gordon, had been born in 1885 — moved to Grafton six months after Fred, arriving on 4 February 1889. The family quickly became involved in the life of the town. Fred (or perhaps his son Freddy) played for Warwicks in the local cricket competition.

Only one of the letters in the Illinois collection dates from Fred's second sojourn in Grafton. It deals mainly with Frank, the son who had been sent to England for his education and who had, it appears, repatriated himself to Australia at the first opportunity by the ingenious stratagem of persuading his grandmother to apprentice him to the sea. All the evidence suggests that his six years in England (1883-89) had been a period of misery for him and of disappointed hopes for his family. He had never been strong and had never shone at his work; but his parents had, as Fred put it in his letter of 20 January 1884

(Letter 20), "made excuses for him" because "the enervating climate of the Clarence made him languid". Similar excuses don't seem to have been made for him at his school at Margate when, as his great-uncle Tom wrote to his uncle Harry (5 April 1886), the climate there proved "too severe . . . for a boy born under Australian skies". Though good accounts of him were occasionally received by his parents, or by great-uncle Tom (who lived in Italy), Fred was constrained to agree with the repeated complaint that he was "idle" and a "sloven". In January 1887, for example, he admitted that he was "awfully" upset by letters from home telling him "how idle" Frank was and added: "I do hope he will have that knocked out of him. He must be taught to work and he cannot begin too young". By this time Frank had presumably started at a public school. When he finished school, in 1889, he announced that he wished to go to sea. His grandmother, according to uncle Harry, was greatly disappointed but acquiesced.[36] By January of 1890, however, he had apparently jumped ship in Australia.

Letter 25   **Grafton**   **27 July 1890**

My dear Mother
    Your last letters or that part of them speaking of Frank made me unhappy and I may say angry especially when you blame Susie for what has taken place. When we first got your letter saying that you had apprenticed Frank and had got over our surpise we determined not to persuade the boy to give up the sea if he liked it, but when we found that he disliked it utterly, I thought then and still do think that it was best he should give it up.
    It had its use as he was then brought face to face with the absolute necessity of choosing an occupation. At first I thought of letting him take a selection. I could have put him on to 1200 acres of good land — but I soon saw he was not fitted for that. He is not one who could quickly adapt himself to the work — neither has he the energy which would make

him successful in that line. In fact like most youngsters he wants supervision, and discipline. The chief Inspector of the Australian Joint Stock Bank is an intimate friend of mine, and at once got him an appointment in Grafton when I asked him.

He joined at £26 per annum to be increased to £50 at the end of six months if he was found efficient. The six months have gone by and he has now got his rise to £50. You say that his occupation is beggardly, but it is surely less so than the sea. The chief prizes are better than any to be got at sea. They have four or five officers at sallaries from £1,000 to £2,500 a year, then they have 200 branches or about 200 and each of these has a manager with salaries ranging from £250 to 700 a year. I am telling you this to show you that the service is not a beggardly one. Of course some get on well and some dont. If Frank sticks steadily to his work for ten years there is no reason why he should not be a manager with a house to live in and a salary of £300 a year besides. That is nothing wonderful but it is a fair prospect, and then as time goes on he improves his position.

I am glad to hear that you let your house in Montague Square. I too have been very much bothered in my own affairs. Though I did fairly well out of mining when I got a good price I sold and now I wish I had not. It has been a very disastrous season for property holders in this coast district, for we have had a succession of floods which have done much damage. I have had no rent since I bought my property on the Macleay nearly a year ago. And I am afraid I may have to go to law with certain trustees from whom I bought to make them make good the title.

There is just a remote chance that an old marriage settlement may prove an impediment, and I insist on having that impediment removed. I have had to fight them on several smaller matters and have got the best of them.

The Rodney has not yet come in. Frank has written to Lawler [?] and to the Sydney agents and send them the bill of lading.

I hope you enjoyed the Passion play.

Your affect. son
Fred Trollope

Frank's defection seems to have brought to the boil a

rivalry that may have been simmering between his mother and his grandmother for a long time. When Frank first arrived in England his relatives there had remarked upon his "Cockney accent" (T.A. Trollope to H.M. Trollope, 24 June 1883) — provoking Fred to reply (6 January 1884) that "It troubles Susie that Frank speaks badly. He certainly was better than that when he was at home". And Fred is, as he puts it, not only "unhappy" but "I may say angry" when his mother blames Susie for Frank's flight back to Australia. He also in effect accuses his mother of having exceeded her authority in "apprenticing" Frank to the sea, a step that had "surprised" his parents. Although his mother was herself the daughter of a bank manager, one suspects that in characterizing Frank's position in the bank as "beggardly" she really means "ungentlemanly". It may or may not be significant that after these strong words between them only one more letter from Fred to his mother survives among the Illinois papers — and that was written nineteen years later. Her grandson Gordon (who wrote to her in 1912 to inform her of his engagement) recorded that she had "hated" Australia and "said many unkind things about it";[37] and her son and his Australian wife presumably knew and resented this.

When Frank's family left Grafton, the year after his return to Australia, he apparently accompanied them. So, according to the shipping list in the *Clarence and Richmond Examiner* (2 June 1891), did a "Mrs Trollope and child", who, if the *Examiner*'s list is correct, must have been either his wife and child or his brother Harry's. But Frank at the time was still only eighteen and Harry seventeen, and according to Debrett neither of them ever married. When Fred made his will in 1897 he named neither Frank nor Harry as his executor but his third son, Frederic Farrand (Freddy), who was also a bank officer.

* * * * *

Barely two years after his return to Grafton, Fred was again "removed" — this time to Hay. It was only then that the full ardour of his new-found affection for Grafton became apparent. His appointment as Chairman of the Land Board at Hay was gazetted on 17 March 1891, but he had left Grafton three weeks earlier. Four days before his departure the *Clarence and Richmond Examiner* had run a story regretting his removal, "for he discharged the duties of his office with much satisfaction; and having been Conditional Purchase Inspector for these districts in former years, he had advantages in administration that qualified him for the position of Chairman above any other that may be appointed from other districts. The sudden action of the department will probably prevent any movement for his retention at Grafton; but we believe that we express public opinion in stating that universal regret will be felt at the change." The Grafton correspondent of the *Clarence River Advocate* (who was quoted in the Hay paper, the *Riverine Grazier*, on 10 March 1891, only a few days after Fred arrived there to take up his new post) was even blunter: "Another absurd action of the . . . Lands Department is the removal of Mr. F.A. Trollope from the extreme north-east position of the colony to its very extreme in the south-west, and I believe the change is not regarded by the official named as a promotion . . . All the experience he had gained in . . . this district [is] cast to the winds . . . If Mr. Trollope had deserved a change, or even been promoted, it would have been different, but as things are it is simply a waste of public money . . ." This public display of insubordination can hardly have endeared Fred to his superiors in Sydney and may explain why he was never "removed" again. The terse comment in his obituary notice in the *Riverine Grazier* nineteen years later indicates that his annoyance persisted: "In 1888 Mr. Trollope found himself again in the Grafton district . . . but he had scarcely comfortably established himself there before he was ordered to Hay in 1890".

Fred left Grafton on 25 February 1891 and reached Hay

six days later, but Susie and the children stayed in Grafton until 30 May.[38] It was not until June that the family was reunited and settled at Czar Lodge, Hay. This was to remain their home until 1903, the twelve years they spent there being the longest period for which they were together as a family. There are no letters written by Fred during this period in the Illinois collection, but the *Riverine Grazier* contains frequent references to the family's activities: advertisements for household help and for a "handy man to mind Garden, Horses, etc."; a Christmas maypole dance at which Effie Trollope (then aged nearly twelve) was one of the children who performed the "Moonlight Serenade"; an unsuccessful appeal by Fred against his assessment for water rates; a banquet for a visiting team from the Melbourne Cricket Club (the "M.C.C. XI") at which Fred was among the guests; donations by Susie to the hospital and the Hay Benevolent Society; Freddy and Harry (then aged seventeen and nineteen respectively) among the candidates for the junior examination "in connection with the Sydney university"; Freddy and Harry (at about the same time) among the stars in the local Australian Rules football competition; Fred serving as president of the Horticultural Society and the Athenaeum Committee and as vice-president of the Cricket Club; "Mrs. Trollope" singing two songs at a concert in aid of the Athenaeum and a member of the family (unspecified) singing in the chorus in the Hay Operatic Society's production of the *Mikado*;[39] Fred making a speech at a farewell banquet for the manager of the local branch of the Commercial Banking Company of Sydney and convening a meeting in the Land Board Office to set up a local branch of the Public Service Association.[40]

On one occasion (15 May 1893) Fred also appeared in court as a prosecution witness, this time with better success than in Wilcannia: "Herbert Tiffin, familiarly known as 'Squizzle', was charged with furious driving on the Hay bridge to the danger of one, to wit, Mr. F. Trollope. . . . Mr F. Trollope was in a buggy with his wife and they had to stop and jump out to save their lives. Accused's actions were those of a madman, and his driving was the most reckless exhibition he had ever witnessed, as the horses were all over the bridge. He could not say if the accused was drunk. Accused fined £5."[41]

When Fred arrived at Hay he was forty-three, and there is every indication that the next ten years or so represented the most satisfying and prosperous phase of his life — at least since his early years at Mortray. Though considerably smaller than Grafton (which had over four thousand people according to the 1901 census, compared with Hay's three thousand), Hay was a great deal bigger than Wilcannia (whose population fell from 1,287 in 1891 to 956 in 1901).

Fred had been in Hay only a month when a letter to the editor of the *Riverine Grazier*, signed "Saltbush" (24 April 1891, p. 2), paid tribute to the liberal spirit in which he was interpreting the land laws, showing that "it is his intention of placing and keeping people on the soil if possible". And his obituary in the same paper nineteen years later ended with an encomium on him as a public official:

> He made hosts of friends throughout the large district which he administered for so long. He was an ideal chairman, having a judicial mind allied to extensive local knowledge of the district and conditions of pastoral occupations. No more just or considerate man ever administered justice. He was fearless in his decisions, and while not being afraid to venture into new paths or to adopt new methods, paid the greatest respect to the experience of the past and was not easily turned aside from adhering to those conditions which had been proved to be of the greatest advantage to the development and occupation of the country. He never forgot in a dry season that there were years of better returns; nor did he fail to remember in the good years that there were recurring periods of drought in Riverina. The testimony of the rain gauge was never absent from his considerations, and the landholders of the Hay Land Board District never had reason to complain that the natural conditions of the country and the disadvantages under which they laboured were not fully taken into

account by the chairman in determining their rental or conditions. It would be difficult to estimate the benefits which have accrued to the Hay Land Board District by the fact that a gentleman of wide experience, an open mind, and the courage of his convictions was entrusted with the administration of the Lands Department during such an important period of the district's history.

In April 1903 Fred began six months' leave of absence, most of which he spent in England. He was farewelled by the local Public Service Association at a "progressive euchre party" during which he received presentations from Land Board members and from other public service groups.[42] None of his family accompanied him to England.[43] Either during his absence or just after his return, Czar Lodge was given up and Susie and the children moved to Sydney, where they again lived at Clavering Cottage.

The obituary in the *Riverine Grazier* attributes their departure from Hay to "the state of Mrs. Trollope's health and the necessity of sending [the] children to Sydney to be educated". Fred's letter of 14 April 1909, the last in the Illinois collection, indicates that Susie was by then suffering from diabetes. She died a few months later.

Letter 26   **Hay**   **14 April 1909**

Dearest Mother

I have yours of 5 March which I found here on my return from a journey the day before yesterday.

I am glad to know that the Girls write to you. Susie I know does at times. I am sorry to say poor Susie is not at all well. That dreadful complaint diabetes punishes her so much. She is much restricted in her food diet and that affects her general health and strength.

Fanny also since the early summer — about November last — has not been well. Some old friends of ours here in Hay invited her to come and spend a month with them for the sake of the change. All was arranged and Fanny was to have left

Sydney last night. But two days before she developed some bad symptoms & had to call in a doctor who ordered her to bed & the Hay trip is postponed. All this is unusual for her, she is generally so splendidly healthy.

I have just finished my southern & western circuit — Deniliquin Moulamein & Balranald — and after sitting for a few days in Hay I will be off on my northern circuit — Hillston and Lake Cadgellico. That will just about take me three weeks. I will then have other work which will keep me busy until the end of June when I hope to get a week in Sydney.

By jove has not the Dreadnought question raised cain in England. Here too it is a burning question. The trouble here is that the Labor party are in power & they do not represent the people. That utter scoundrel Deakin & the Victorian protectionists allied themselves with the Labor party to bring in protection. The Labor party dont care what is done so long as the Labor people gain something — or *think* they gain something — Then when it suits them they oust Deakin & just at this time the navy question — the huge big navy question — comes up, & while three fourths of Australia want to join in contributing to the defence of the Empire, this twopenny Labor crowd who are in power by accident wont join in.

However the people will take the matter out of the hands of the Government. They — the Gov: — have to meet parliament in May. That utter traitor Deakin may with his band of Victorian protectionists join with the Government & save their miserable skins until the next general election. But if so the separate states who thank heavens have a revenue independent of the Commonwealth will act and will support the old country.

With us the Catholics are often disloyal — individually the Labor men are loyal, collectively they are not loyal, but the great body of the people are as loyal as if they belonged to an English county.

The Labor party are an anomaly. They pretend to think they can govern without respect of any interests except their own. They are utterly, entirely & hopelessly selfish, & they cannot long continue to exist.

They have been successful so far as their followers will vote solidly for the men they put up & the parties against them are not solid. But they cannot govern — the question is what harm will they do until they are extinguished. There is no argument with them. They have no sense of right & wrong. It is what they want or rather what they *think* they want.

I have not heard from Frank since his arrival at his new house, but expect to shortly.

Goodbye darling Mother
Your affect. son
Fred Trollope

In the absence of any other letters written from Hay there is no way of knowing whether Fred and Susie found the climate there any less debilitating than that of Grafton. It may be significant, however, that on at least two occasions — both in midsummer — Fred arranged temporary transfers to cooler places (Orange in January 1897 and Armidale in January 1906).[44] One is also struck by the remark in his obituary that when he first went to Grafton in 1877 — after finding Goulburn too cold — "The change of climate greatly benefitted him": the affection which had so surprisingly effaced his initial hatred of Grafton had apparently intensified on the parched plains of the Riverina.

Fred's violent diatribe against the Labor Party and against Alfred Deakin, the leader of the Protectionist party, over the Dreadnought crisis, exhibits much the same mixture of anti-protectionism and jingoism as his earlier letter on the Home Rule question (14). But superadded to this mixture is a snarling Tory arrogance which his father, even after his own political conversion, would surely have deplored — along with the jingoism and imperialism. A few months after the letter was written Deakin abandoned Andrew Fisher's Labor government and himself became prime minister, with the support of his former opponents, the free traders. But the Labor party, far from ceasing to exist (as Fred had predicted), won office on its own at the election the following year.

It is clear from his letter that even while he was at Hay Fred's work entailed a great deal of travelling. The year before (1908) he had twice been relieved of his duties, presumably because of ill health, and his health appears to have broken down again early in June, before he had completed the work that was to have kept him busy until the end of that month. On 28 July he was described in the New South Wales Government Gazette as already on leave of absence because of ill health and was relieved of his position as Chairman of the Hay Land Board. His retirement from the Public Service was gazetted on 9 March 1910, to take effect from 10 February 1910. He died on 31 May 1910. A short obituary notice appeared in the *Sydney Morning Herald*, which also listed some of the more prominent mourners at his funeral. Both his daughters and all but one of his sons were present.

At the time of Fred's death none of his sons were married, but in 1907 his elder daughter Fanny had married Wilfred Meillon, manager of a bank at Hay, and his youngest son, Gordon Clavering, wrote to his grandmother in 1912 (8 March) to announce his engagement to Mary Blacket. Gordon and Mary were married in 1913, and later resided at Roseville, Sydney in another Trollopian "cottage", Framley. Frank, Harry, and Freddy all remained unmarried. Freddy eventually inherited the family baronetcy, after a number of relatives who had stood between him and the title had died or been killed in the first world war. From him the titled passed to Gordon, whose elder son Anthony is the present baronet. After Fred's death those of the children who were still at home moved to another Clavering Cottage, in Shirley Street, Wollstonecraft. The present baronet lives at yet another Clavering — in Roseville. Their great ancestor would no doubt be amused, and pleased, to find a corner of Barset surviving on Sydney's North Shore.[45]

* * * * *

I said before that Frederic Trollope was unmistakably

his father's son. The likeness is evident in all sorts of ways, not least in his prose-style and even his calligraphy; it also reveals itself, to some extent, in his literary tastes. In one of the earliest of the Illinois letters (Letter 2, to his brother Harry) he enclosed a poem composed by a lawyer in Forbes, and his obituary in the *Riverine Grazier* devotes a paragraph to his meetings with another poet, Henry Kendall, during the period when Kendall was living at Camden Haven — since re-named Kendall — and Fred was stationed at Grafton: the meetings presumably occurred during the period 1877-81. Fred (or rather the author of the obituary notice) described his acquaintance with Kendall as one of the "pleasanter recollections" of that phase of his life, remarking that Kendall "was not always in good health, but when in the vein was a charming companion". In Letter 7 (1881) he also reported his meeting, on a trip to the Mudgee-Dubbo district, with an Australian writer who, within a few years, was to become even more famous than Kendall, Rolf Boldrewood. His letters show that he read his father's novels, and his long complaint, in Letter 18 (1884), about the *Times* review of Anthony's *Autobiography* is pure Trollopian in tone and style — though Anthony would have squirmed a little at Fred's praise of the *Autobiography* as a "most charming" piece of writing.

Like his father, Fred was a public servant for most of his working life, and to find a parallel to the imperious condescension which characterizes his private comments on his official superiors, and which issued in one period of extreme exasperation as publicly proclaimed contempt for them, we have only to turn to the passages in Anthony's *Autobiography* in which he licks his lips over the "delicious feuds" he engaged in as a post-office employee and the delight he took in differing with Sir Rowland Hill at every opportunity. Like his father, Fred seems to have been vociferous in argument, irascible and impatient with underlings and members of his family, but capable in his more temperate moments of unusual compassion and fair-mindedness. The testimonies to his judicial patience and sympathy as a Land Board chairman are too warm to be explained away as mere formal eulogy. But neither can one altogether disregard the evidence of "imperiousness", of a perhaps slightly cranky love of litigation, and of haughty censoriousness, particularly towards his peers in the Lands Office (whose bureaucratic sloth, as pictured in Letter 16, seems little different from that which Anthony had so lovingly evoked in his semi-autobiographical novel *The Three Clerks*). His disapproval of his "idle" eldest son also strikes one as rather savage — even by Victorian standards; and the fact that so few of his children, and none of the three eldest sons, ever married inevitably invites conjecture about their relationship with a father who may (like his own father) have been over-heavy at times and a mother whose constant ill-health and pregnancies may have weakened her capacity to give emotional support to her children (or who may, alternatively, have established an emotional nexus between them and herself as a sanctuary from the severity of her husband). Anthony himself had only two children and, on all the evidence, a strong-minded wife; he also achieved fame, wealth, and independence to compensate him for the tortures of his childhood and early manhood. Fred by contrast suffered the continual anxieties of providing for a large family in a succession of disagreeable climates, with a physically exhausting job that for the last twenty years offered no real prospect of promotion, and with the stability of his family life dependent on the whim of official superiors. Doubtless the shadow of his famous father, and the recollection of his own early failure to establish himself as a country gentleman, also threw a little gloom over his later years. By colonial standards his was certainly not a life of unusual vicissitude or hardship, but it was by no means easy or comfortable, and his letters suggest that it left him at heart disappointed and unsatisfied.

Notes

1. Mary Lazarus, *A Tale of Two Brothers* (Sydney: Angus and Robertson, 1973), p. 92. Mary Lazarus also notes (pp. 52-53) that in the early 1870s Alfred Dickens and Frederic Trollope had occupied neighbouring sheep stations near Forbes, New South Wales.
2. Manuscript letter from Thomas Adolphus Trollope to Henry M. Trollope, 18 March 1885; in University of Illinois Library.
3. Shipping list in the *Argus* (Melbourne), 18 December 1865, p. 4. Fred travelled on the *Madras*.
4. Anthony Trollope, *An Autobiography* (World's Classics, 1980), p. 326.
5. *Riverine Grazier* (Hay, New South Wales), 7 June 1910, p. 2.
6. Shipping list in the *Argus*, 13 July 1869, p. 4. Fred had travelled to England on the *Great Britain*, which left Melbourne on 8 October 1868 (*Argus*, 8 October 1868, p. 4).
7. See P.D. Edwards and R.B. Joyce, ed., Anthony Trollope's *Australia* (St Lucia: University of Queensland Press, 1967), p. 350ff. and Editors' Introduction, pp. 19-20.
8. The murdered man was James ("Rarey") Ashton, an employee on a sheep station called Kangorooby owned by a Mr Glasson. Ashton's decomposed body was discovered on 29 October 1872. At the inquest, held on 2 November 1872, three men (James Sheridan, James Field, and George Lowrie) were committed for trial. See *Sydney Morning Herald*, 5 November 1872, p. 5; 16 November 1872, p. 5.
9. The "old house", which the family had occupied since 1859, was Waltham House, Waltham Cross, Herts. Early in 1873, after their return from Australia, Anthony and his wife took a house at 39 Montagu Square, where they remained until 1880.
10. Bradford Allen Booth, ed., *The Letters of Anthony Trollope* (London: O.U.P., 1951), p. 295. Alfred Dickens's subsequent career is traced in Mary Lazarus's *A Tale of Two Brothers*.
11. Lewes's letters are included in G.S. Haight, ed., *The George Eliot Letters* (London: O.U.P., 1956), 5, pp. 351, 357.
12. Shipping lists in *Sydney Morning Herald*, 22 February 1873, p. 6, and 14 July 1873, p. 4.
13. *Harry Heathcote of Gangoil* was first published as the Christmas 1873 number of the *Graphic* (London). It was then issued as a book, in one volume, by Sampson Low in 1874. It was republished by Lansdowne Press, Melbourne in 1963 and by Arno Press, N.Y. in 1981, with an introduction by P.D. Edwards.
14. Shepherd Smith had been General Manager of the Bank of New South Wales since 1864.
15. On Hay, see my comments following Letter 4.
16. William Bede Dalley, distinguished politician, barrister, and journalist. He had been Attorney General of New South Wales at the time of Anthony Trollope's second visit to the colony (1875).
17. See Trollope's *Australia*, pp. 238,n.2-239; *Sydney Morning Herald*, 26 August 1875, p. 4 and 7 August 1875, pp. 6-7.
18. The new house, into which Fred's parents moved in July 1880, was at Harting, near Petersfield, Sussex.

19. Anthony Trollope's novel *Dr. Wortle's School* was published in two volumes in January 1881. Fred was probably reading the serialization in *Blackwood's* (May-December 1880). The chapter, "Nobody has condemned you here" (part 5, chapter 7), appeared in November 1880.
20. See Rolf Boldrewood, *The Miner's Right*, chapter 41; Trollope's *Australia*, pp. 296n.-297n.; and R.B. Walker, "History and Fiction in Rolf Boldrewood's *The Miner's Right*", *Australian Literary Studies*, 3 (June 1967): 28-40.
21. Anthony Trollope's novel *The Fixed Period* is set in the newly independent colony of Britannula in the late twentieth century. It was serialized in *Blackwood's*, October 1881-March 1882.
22. The Minister for Lands resigned in November 1881. Robertson officially replaced him from 29 December 1881. Sir Henry Parkes, the Premier, was in England.
23. Presumably in 1868: see note 6 above.
24. *The Letters of Anthony Trollope*, p. 483.
25. Fred is referring to the "Kilmainham Treaty" (1881), under which Parnell and other leaders of the National Land League, who had been imprisoned for incitement to violence, were released from gaol.
26. Arabi Pasha led the Egyptian revolt against Anglo-French suzerainty in 1882. The revolt was finally crushed, at Tel-el-Kebir, eight days after Fred's letter was written.
27. Wilcannia, where Fred was stationed later, was also agitating for a railway line — like Grafton, unsuccessfully.
28. Probably the obituary in the *Sydney Morning Herald*, 9 December 1882, p. 7.
29. Two articles on the *Autobiography* appeared in the *Times*, the first on 12 October 1883, p. 10, the second on 13 October 1883, p. 8.
30. Trollope strenuously defended *The Prime Minister* (1876) in his *Autobiography*, pp. 360n., 362n.
31. *Orley Farm* (1862) was also one of Anthony Trollope's favourites among his novels: see his *Autobiography*, pp. 166-67.
32. See Trollope's *Australia*, p. 596n. and Augustus J.C. Hare, *The Story of My Life* (1896), 1, chapter 1.
33. See Mary Lutyens, *Millais and the Ruskins* (N.Y.: Vanguard Press, 1967), p. 182n., and Sir William James, *The Order of Release* (London: John Murray, 1948), p. 13.
34. The novel, surely one of the dullest ever written, was called *My Own Love-Story*, 2 vols (London: Chapman and Hall, 1887).
35. Thomas Adolphus Trollope ("Uncle Tom") wrote novels and travel-books but signally failed to emulate the literary fame and success of his mother Frances and his brother Anthony. Unlike Anthony, he never had to work for his living but was supported by his mother. He lived for most of his adult life at Florence. His letters to Fred's brother Harry — in the University of Illinois collection — suggest that in his old age, if not before, he was selfish, demanding, even somewhat sybaritic. Fred's question, "but what has he done for his pension?" probably reflects a general resentment towards him on the part of Anthony and his family.
36. Letter from Thomas Adolphus Trollope to Henry Merivale Trollope, 31 December 1889 (in University of Illinois Library).

37. Gordon Trollope, "Trollope in Australia", *The Bulletin* (Sydney), 2 April 1930, p. 5.
38. Shipping lists in *Clarence and Richmond Examiner*, 28 February 1891, p. 4 and 2 June 1891, p. 2.
39. Fred's son Gordon recalled that Anthony Trollope, during his visits to Australia, "used to love to sit and hear [Susie] sing" and that "some of the lovely songs of the day" that Anthony gave her were "still in existence" in 1930. (Gordon Trollope, "Trollope in Australia".)
40. *Riverine Grazier*, 23 June 1891, p. 3, 8 September 1891, p. 3, 18 December 1891, p. 2, 12 February 1892, p. 2, 22 April 1892, p. 2, 22 December 1891, p. 4, 2 August 1892, p. 2, 13 September 1892, p. 2, 20 September 1892, p. 4, 18 September 1894, p. 2, 7 July 1893, p. 2, 27 October 1893, p. 2, 15 September 1893, p. 2, 5 December 1899, p. 2.
41. *Riverine Grazier*, 16 May 1893, p. 2.
42. *Riverine Grazier*, 25 March 1903, p. 2. The paper reported Fred's return to Hay on 30 October 1903, p. 2.
43. Shipping lists in *Sydney Morning Herald*, 9 April 1903, p. 9 and 13 October 1903, p. 8.
44. *N.S.W. Government Gazette*, 20 January 1897, p. 391 and 10 January 1906, p. 215.
45. Framley Cottage and Clavering Cottage took their names from Anthony Trollope's novels *Framley Parsonage* (1861) and *The Claverings* (1867); both novels are set in Barsetshire, the "dear county" that Trollope invented.

Index

Albury (NSW), 44
Arabi Pasha, 32, 64 n.26
Armidale (NSW), 59
Ashton, James (murder victim), 6, 63 n.8
Australia [and New Zealand] (by Anthony Trollope), 3, 15, 22, 63 n.17
Australian Club (Sydney), 11, 16
Australian Joint Stock Bank, 52
Autobiography, An (by Anthony Trollope), 3, 4, 12-13, 22, 40, 64 n.30, 61

Badham, Dr Charles, 14-15
Balranald (NSW), 21, 58
Bank of NSW, 11-14, 17
Barratta station, 4
Bathurst (NSW), 6, 21, 48
Bingara (NSW), 16
Blacket, Mary (m. Gordon Trollope), 60
Blackwood's Magazine, 7, 24, 64 n.19
Bland, Florence, 17, 32, 41, 47
Blythe, Mr (commissioner, Lands Department), 26, 30
Bolding, Mr (commissioner, Lands Department), 26
Boldrewood, Rolf (T.A. Browne), 21, 22, 61, 64 n.20
Booroondara East Station, 15-17
Bourke (NSW), 47, 49
Bowen, Sir George, 12-13

Casino (NSW), 49
Churchill, Lord Randolph, 48-49
Claverings, The (by Anthony Trollope), 65 n.45
Clough, I.H., 7, 8
Cobar (NSW), 15
Corowa (NSW), 43-45
Cramner, Mr (?), 16

Dally, W.B., 12, 63 n.16
Davies, Mary, 31, 64 n.24
Davis, Mr (barrister), 14
Deakin, Alfred, 58-59
Deniliquin (NSW), 4, 49, 58
Dickens, A.T.D., 1, 63 n.1, 5, 63 n.7
Dickens, Charles, 1, 63 n.1
Dickens, E.B.L., 1, 63 n.1
Doctor Wortle's School (by Anthony Trollope), 19, 64 n.19
Dubbo (NSW), 20-21, 61

Field, James, 6, 63 n.8
Fisher, Andrew, 59
Fixed Period, The (by Anthony Trollope), 24, 64 n.21
Forbes (NSW), 6, 9, 16, 61
Framley Parsonage (by Anthony Trollope), 65 n.45

Gibson, Mr (squatter), 16
Gilchrist, Watt and Co., 11-14
Glen Innes (NSW), 19
Goulburn (NSW), 18-59
Grafton (NSW), 18-35, 37, 41, 43, 46, 49-55, 56, 59, 61

Gray, George, 44-45
Gray, John, 44-45, 64 n.33
Grenfell (NSW), 4
Gulgong (NSW), 21, 22, 63 n.20

Hare, Augustus J.C., 64 n.32
Hare, Francis, 44-45
Hare, G.E.C., 45
Hare, Julius, 44-45
Hare, Reginald, 44-45
Harrow School, 21, 22
Harry Heathcote of Gangoil (by Anthony Trollope), 10, 63 n.13
Harting (Sussex), 36, 63 n.18
Hartington, Lord, 48-49
Hawkesbury River (NSW), 15
Hay (NSW), 3, 54-60
Hay, William, 12, 63 n.15, 15
Hill, Sir Rowland, 61
Hillston (NSW), 58
Hill End (NSW), 6

Inverell (NSW), 15-16, 19
Ireland, 32-33

Jennings, Sir Patrick, 14, 15

Kater, Mr, 12
Kempsey (NSW), 19
Kendall, Henry, 61

Labor Party, 58-59
Lake Cargellico (NSW), 58
Landleaguers, The (by Anthony Trollope), 32-33
Landor, W.S., 45
Last Chronicle of Barset, The (by Anthony Trollope), 22
Lazarus, Mary, 1, 64 n.1
Lewes, G.H., 10, 63 n.10
Lismore (NSW), 49
Lord, Mr (Inspector of Conditional Purchases), 16
Lowrie, George, 6, 63 n.8

Macleay River (NSW), 19, 37, 52
Manning River (NSW), 29-30
Margate, 51
Martin, Sir James, 14, 15
Meillon, Wilfred (Fred's son-in-law), 60

Melbourne, 2, 4, 7, 8, 11, 28
Melbourne Cricket Club ("MCC"), 55
Millais, Effie (née Gray), 45
Millais, J.E., 44-45
Mining, 5, 8-9
Moriarty, A.O., 20, 22, 33-34
Mortray station, 4-14, 48, 56
Moulamein (NSW), 58
Mudgee (NSW), 20-21, 22, 61
Murwillumbah (NSW), 49

Orange (NSW), 59
Orley Farm (by Anthony Trollope), 40, 64 n.31

Parkes, Sir Henry, 25, 27, 64 n.22
Parnell, Charles Stewart, 32, 64 n.25
Plunket, Mr (under secretary for Justice), 20
Port Macquarie (NSW), 19, 29
Port Stephens (NSW), 19
Prime Minister, The (by Anthony Trollope), 40, 64 n.30

Railways (in NSW), 32, 39, 42, 64 n.27
Richmond River (NSW), 24, 26, 37, 44
Robertson, Sir John, 20, 21, 27, 64 n.22
Robinson, Sir Hercules, 12-13, 17
Robinson, Miss, 16
Ruskin, John, 45
Russell, H.S., 21, 22

Salisbury, Lord, 48-49
Saturday Review, The, 6-7
Sheridan, James, 6, 63 n.8
Slade, Mr (lawyer), 14
Smith, Shepherd, 11, 63 n.14, 12, 13-14
Sydney, 9, 10, 11-12, 13-15, 16, 18, 19-20, 27-28, 33-46, 52, 57, 58

Taree (NSW), 29-30
Tenterfield (NSW), 19
Three Clerks, The (by Anthony Trollope), 62
Trollope, Ada (Fred's sister-in-law), 48

Trollope, Anthony (Fred's father), *passim* letters to, 11-12, 13-14, 15-17, 18-19; books by. See under individual titles

Trollope, Arthur John ("Jack"; Fred's fourth son), 24, 25, 30-31, 32

Trollope, Clive (Fred's fifth son), 35

Trollope, Effie Madeleine (Fred's second daughter), 30, 32, 55, 57, 60

Trollope, Frances Kathleen (Fred's elder daughter; m. Meillon), 30, 40, 57-58, 60

Trollope, Frank Anthony (Fred's eldest son), 5, 8, 17, 19, 21, 22-24, 26, 31, 35-36, 38, 39, 40, 43, 44, 46, 47, 48, 50-53, 59, 60, 62

Trollope, Frederic Farrand (Fred's third son), 17, 40, 50, 53, 55, 60, 62

Trollope, Gordon Clavering (Fred's youngest son), 50, 53, 60, 65 n.37 and n.39

Trollope, Harry (Fred's second son), 17, 23, 26, 40, 53, 55, 60, 62

Trollope, Henry Merivale ("Harry"; Fred's brother), 3, 6, 7, 8-10, 12, 33, 35-36, 47-49, 51, 53; letters to, 8-9, 48-49, 63 n.2, 64 n.36

Trollope, Muriel Rose (Fred's niece), 47-48

Trollope, Rose (Fred's mother), *passim* letters to, 5-7, 24-25, 28, 29-30, 30-31, 33-34, 35-36, 38-39, 39-40, 41, 42-43, 44, 45, 46-47, 51-52, 57-59

Trollope, Thomas Adolphus (Fred's uncle), 2, 3, 48, 64 n.35, 51, 53, 63, 64 n.36

Waltham House (Waltham Cross, Herts.), 6, 63 n.9
Warbreccan station, 15
Warialda (NSW), 16
Warragamba (NSW), 15
Wilcannia (NSW), 1-2, 46-49, 55, 56, 64 n.27
Wilkinson, Robert, 20, 21-22
Winchester College, 44-45

YMCA, 30